"This book will help you understand the basics of Bitcoin, and will pay for itself again and again. Yuri and Steve answer the $250,000 question on why you don't want to be left behind."

—Timothy Draper, Founder, Draper Associates & DFJ

"Understanding and using cryptocurrencies is daunting for anyone, simply because it's a new way to interact and trade money and value. This book takes complex ideas, makes them understandable to a non-expert and therefore useful for someone seeking more information on the evolving digital assets space."

—Thomas J. Lee, CFA, Co-Founder and Head of Research,
FUNDSTRAT Global Advisors

"Bitcoin and blockchain have sparked a global disruption of traditional industries that's changing the game faster than anything we've witnessed in modern history. This book teaches you the rules so you can play to win!"

—Brock J. Pierce, Chairman, The Bitcoin Foundation

"Simply the best introduction to cryptocurrency out there. It's simple, concise and reader friendly. Read and share this book or you might Be Left Behind."

—Bob Raffo, CEO, FirstView Financial and PayTech Leader

"Bitcoin demystified! Yuri and Steve have given us a complex topic and turned it into a book that anyone can read and understand."

—Ott Velsberg, Chief Data Scientist, Ministry of Economic
Affairs and Communications, Republic of Estonia

D0924635

"Steve and Yuri think from a customer's perspective – sorely needed when explaining blockchain! What might the reader be interested in? What might confuse the reader? How best to help the reader understand a difficult and sprawling topic? ELI5: Explain Like I'm 5 years old. This book is both engaging and enlightening."

—Arne Hessenbruch, Lecturer in Innovation at MIT

"Steve and Yuri have written THE crypto and Bitcoin book that everyone has been waiting for. They make the boring fun and the complex simple so that no one will be left behind."

—Herbert R. Sim, TheBitcoinMan.com

"Steve and Yuri do a great job of arming you with the arsenal you need to start your quest into the blockchain revolution that's coming to shake this world at its core."

—Robert Beadles, Co-Founder, The Monarch Wallet

"This book is a fantastic primer that newcomers and veterans alike should not only read, but share with others. Cryptocurrencies are wildly speculative and it's still a new frontier, a Wild West if you will. This book is your horse and six shooter that will help you survive."

—Jason Appleton, Crypto Crow

"An electrifying book about the future of money. If you are not inspired to rethink your whole approach to ownership rights and identity, start again on page one."

—Panos A Panay, Senior Vice President,
Global Strategy and Innovation, Berklee College of
Music, co-founder Open Music Initiative

"*Be Left Behind* provides a practical introduction to using cryptocurrencies which emphasizes the ever-changing regulatory landscape. Great read for a how-to overview guide."

—Barrett Strickland, Head of Analytics and Research, TokenTax

"This book manages to take one of the most complex new fields in technology and explain it in a simple, digestible format for any reader. It prioritizes enabling newcomers and mass adoption above all else, which is a huge service to the industry."

—Faizan J. Khan, Founder, Managing Director at Visary Capital

BE LEFT BEHIND

DISCOVER BITCOIN AND CRYPTOCURRENCY

BEFORE YOUR GRANDMA BEATS YOU TO IT

STEVE GOOD AND YURI CATALDO

SmartWhalePress

Disclaimer

Be Left Behind is a book about Bitcoin, cryptocurrency and blockchain. Although we're generally bullish on the future of Bitcoin and cryptocurrency, this book is not giving you any investing advice. We're not financial advisors, nor is our publishing house, and we don't know you or any of our readers personally. The book is not intended to serve the purpose of advising you, but as a generalized commentary and opinion as authors, not as financial advisors. Please seek individual advice if you are looking to make an investment decision. Please see our disclaimer and disclosures page on our website for additional information and any updates.

www.beleftbehind.com/disclaimer.

Copyright © 2020 Steve Good and Yuri Cataldo

All right reserved. No part of this publication may be produced, stored in a retrieval system, or transmitted, in any form or by any means, electronic, mechanical, photocopying, recording or otherwise, without the prior permission of the publishers.

Printed in the United Kingdom and the United States of America.

Smart Whale Press
61 Bridge Street
Kington, Hertfordshire, HR5 3DJ
United Kingdom
www.smartwhalepress.com

First Edition: January 2020
10 9 8 7 6 5 4 3 2 1

Cover Design by Ivan Bliminse
Interior Layout by S. Peter Lewis
Interior Graphics Design by Paulii Good

Library of Congress Card Number: 2019921019
A record of this book is held in the Estonian National Library

ISBN: 978-9949-01-632-7
ISBN: 978-9949-7437-0-4
ISBN: 978-1712-8365-1-4

www.beleftbehind.com

Dedication

To my amazing boys, Xander and Dylan, you have taught me how to understand cryptocurrency from a young person's point of view and have been my amazing support team during this incredible journey. And to my wife, Paulii, you have been my incredible rock during the long hours, nights, and weekends I spent with Yuri instead of you! -Steve

To my loving parents, Giuseppe and Aksana, who always encouraged me to reach for the stars. *Semper tibi amo.* -Yuri

About the Authors

Steve Good

Steve Good is a digital strategist, entrepreneur and public speaker who consults with companies to help them drive their growth. He also focusses on raising awareness and adoption in blockchain and cryptocurrency. He spent more than 20 years in Financial Services and Technology as a Management Consultant and Client Account Manager at Deloitte and Infosys before dedicating his time to blockchain and cryptocurrency. He's an accomplished entrepreneur with board level experience, a public figure, keynote speaker, and has been featured in numerous articles including BuzzFeed and How-To Geek. He currently resides in London, United Kingdom with his family.

Yuri Cataldo

Yuri Cataldo advises companies on public relations, marketing, and media strategy. Named one of Forty under 40 business leaders in Indiana, he's an award-winning entrepreneur, and Yale-trained designer with credits on Broadway. He founded the three-time international award-winning bottled water company, IndigoH2O, and has been featured in various media outlets including Inc., *Forbes*, and The Boston Globe. He has guest lectured at Yale, MIT, Tufts, Princeton, and Stanford, as well as conferences throughout the world on the topics of the future of work, creative entrepreneurship, and innovation. He currently lives in Boston, Massachusetts, USA.

Acknowledgements

This book wouldn't be possible without our amazing friends who have supported us over the years on this epic journey of getting started in Bitcoin, cryptocurrency, and blockchain.

David Nguyen, whose initial prodding got the ball rolling with *The Coin Chat*, and ultimately led to this book.

Paulii Good, who has been our amazing secret weapon, working tirelessly behind the scenes on all our marketing and creating the amazing graphics for our book.

Joe Wasson, who was instrumental in helping us understand the technical aspects and how to keep your coins safe and secure.

Chas Gesner, Kyle Burford, Mike Ruskow, Shawn Erikson, Allison Mitchell, Jessica McCormack, Brigham Santos, Patrick Ryan, Bo Gulledge, Jeremy Austin, Bo Henriksen, Iris Xu, Poppy Deng, Marina Petrichenko, David Atkinson, Gillian Godsil, David Schwartz, Tina Fotherby, Sheila Trask, Ryan Dempsey, Ann Sheybani, and all of our friends and family who took the time to read manuscript drafts and provide feedback to make this book even better.

Our deepest gratitude and appreciation to all of you!

And special thanks to our amazing supporters and subscribers to our show, The Coin Chat — you have helped us shape the content we have today.

We would also like to acknowledge a number of other major influencers (not necessarily mentioned within the book) who are all found on Twitter, many of whom have helped us with minor reviews, feedback and comments. All of them are people worth checking out.

- Anthony Pompliano (@APompliano)
- Mark W. Yusko (@MarkYusko)
- Tim Draper (@TimDraper)
- Thomas J. Lee (@fundstrat)
- Brock Pierce (@brockpierce)
- Andreas Antonopoulos (@aantonop)
- Bobby Lee (@bobbyclee)
- Tone Vays (@ToneVays)
- Crypto Sara (@altcoinsara)
- Herbert R. Sim—TheBitcoinMan (@HerbertRSim)
- Bruce Porter, Jr (@NetworksManager)
- Steve McGarry (@stvmcg)
- Ben Armstrong (@BitBoy_Crypto)

Check out our website for a list of influencers at www.beleftbehind.com/influencers

CONTENTS

FOREWORD

Great technology should be beautiful or invisible all together. However, to appreciate the true beauty of something as invisible as Bitcoin, or all digital/cryptocurrencies for that matter, one must begin to understand what it is, why we need it, and what it could mean for us.

The authors of this book are what I call ELI5. This is not technical jargon. ELI5 simply means, "Explain Like I am 5." If you haven't already, I highly encourage you to view the videos put out by Steve and Yuri—especially the video where Steve gets his five-year-old to explain blockchain. Watching this after a few drinks at a conference engaged me and I felt the authors were onto something with their planned book. I understood over the course of the evening the genuineness of their collective interest in helping pull forward the wide masses being left behind.

While you don't need to be a rocket scientist to be an astronaut or a mechanical engineer to drive a car, it's good to understand the basics of the vehicle you're getting into and how it can take you to destinations that have been out of reach until now. This is what this book is about.

While there are many books out there, none try to be as genuinely interested in educating the reader in an effective manner. *Be Left Behind* will ensure you get the basics in order and be ready to take the plunge into the future. Watching from the sidelines could be fun; plunging in might be a roller coaster ride—just be best equipped to make the decision that's right for you. Read the book to decide which side of the fence you'll be on.

Remember, global wealth is estimated at hundreds of trillions of dollars. As an increasing amount of people and financial institutions replace traditional assets like gold with Bitcoin as their (long-term) store of value, the potential price levels are mind-boggling. I have gone on record to predict over $60 thousand in five years. Others predict as much as $1 million for a Bitcoin in the longer term.

In other words, we're looking at something of a financial revolution.

Revolutions and disruptions may be technology-enabled, but they're always people led. If you have picked up this book you have taken the first step towards joining one of the most defining revolutions of our generation—one that will change almost every aspect of the financial lives we live today. Congratulations!

I have been in this space for 20 years now. "This space" being largely defined as digital currencies, encryption, and financial decentralization. I released my first digital currency in 1999; however, it wasn't blockchain-based, and the world was largely unaware of the need for a digital online currency.

Then, in 2007, I wrote the paper on financial decentralization and how we can make any market in this world a people-only market by removing any and all intermediaries. It's a lofty goal, but one increasingly appreciated by people around the world: one person in the system can now become sovereign, with full control of all aspects of his life, interactions, data, and finances.

Around the time the Bitcoin team decided to publish their whitepaper, I completed the financial decentralization paper and went a different route. With cryptocurrencies such as Bitcoin one of the key pillars of financial decentralization, I decided to focus on the other two pillars: multi-party settlements and algorithms that help recreate efficient market dynamics without any centralized agencies.

This is a brave new world, and yet in many ways, you're about to enter established territory. Some of us are comfortably at home here and can teach you to be too. By reading this book, you can be sure you will not be left behind on the dry dock while other savvy souls take the plunge.

I, for one, am proud to be associated with the book and happy to have been able to contribute my sarcasm to the title. Having been in this space for almost two decades, I can tell you this book is a must read for anyone just starting out. We never had the benefit of such a helpful resource when we started out. But you do. This book may be a small step in financial literacy, but one that could mean a giant leap for anyone reading it with intent. Will you read it? Or, you know . . . just be left behind?

Vaibhav Kadikar
Founder and CEO, CloseCross
Inventor of the multi-party settlement mechanism and author of *Knowledge Value of Time Algorithms*
1/5

CHAPTER ONE

AN INTRO TO CRYPTOCURRENCY

We know you're here to learn about cryptocurrency and Bitcoin, but we might as well have a bit of fun in the process. So, here's a trivia question to get you thinking (we'll come back to it later):

What's the one alternative currency you loved, especially as a child?

While you're thinking about that, let's ease you into the topic at hand. Right now, cryptocurrency may feel like an incomprehensible world, especially when you're just getting started. We've been there. We've experienced the whole process of learning how to buy, send, spend, and invest in cryptocurrency, so we know how frustrating and confusing it can be.

When you're first starting out, there can be a ton of questions about how to get into blockchain and cryptocurrency:

- How do I get started?
- What is Bitcoin?
- How do I buy and spend Bitcoin?
- Is Bitcoin safe?
- How do I keep my data safe and private?

- What's the difference between blockchain and cryptocurrency?

- What's the difference between cryptocurrency and coins?

- Is it all a giant pyramid or Ponzi scheme?

- How do I spot a scam and avoid losing my money?

- How do I store my coins and keep them safe?

- Should I invest?[1]

If you don't yet know the answers to these questions you're not alone—most people can't answer a single one. People are intimidated by cryptocurrency and think it's too complicated to wrap their heads around, so they give up. Even worse, some feel the cryptocurrency craze has already passed them by, so they don't even try to get started.

We're here to tell you, it's not too complicated to learn and nothing has passed you by. As a matter of fact, by the end of this book, you're going to feel a whole lot more confident than you do right now; in fact, we're sure you're going to want to get more involved. Don't worry, you won't be left behind, certainly not if we can help it.

We're about to cover a wide range of topics, with enough information and tips to get you started. As we dig into each topic, you'll not only have the latest buzzwords at your disposal, you'll begin to feel comfortable using them too.

We've written this book as your one-stop shop for everything blockchain, cryptocurrency, and coin-related. Stick with us, just like thousands of our followers do, and you'll understand the difference between these concepts; you'll also learn how you can send, buy, spend, invest, and keep your coins safe.

---

1 Remember, we're authors, not financial advisors. See Disclaimer

More importantly, by the time you're done reading this book, you'll understand enough to make a more informed decision about how to buy Bitcoin and cryptocurrency in general, as well as how to keep your coins and your privacy safe.

Before we go any further, let's see how these concepts really aren't as new as you might think.

ALTERNATIVE CURRENCIES: THEN AND NOW

You may think alternative currencies aren't "real"; at the very least, they're hard to grasp. That's understandable. We're familiar and comfortable with currencies created by governments. But what if we told you the idea of alternative currencies isn't new?

Alternative currencies have been around for hundreds of years.

One of the most common alternative currencies is bartering. Yes, that's correct. Bartering is a form of currency: exchanging goods and services for other goods and services. Bartering was one of the first forms of economic exchange. In fact, we still use this alternative currency today. Airline miles and other loyalty programs are modern forms of bartering.

Here are some other unusual and interesting alternative currencies (as you'll see, some are more reputable than others):

- In 2013, New York magazine ran an article called "Suds for Drugs." It explained how gangs were stealing Tide soap detergent from large grocery stores and trading it with drug dealers for crack cocaine. Drug dealers would then sell the Tide to small local shops for cash (who got it cheaper this way than from wholesalers). Since Tide detergent is an expensive item and readily available, it became a convenient method of barter that gave everyone what they wanted (drugs or money). What started in a small neighborhood just outside of Washington,

D.C., became the number one retail shoplifted item across the United States.

- The WIR Franc is an alternative currency, created by the WIR Bank in Switzerland in 1934, for trade between businesses. It was started by businessmen Werner Zimmerman and Paul Enz as a result of the currency shortage due to the global financial instability of the time. Zimmerman and Enz actually ended up getting a banking license in 1936. WIR currency still exists today; it started with only sixteen members, and now boasts over 62,000, with total assets of around three billion Swiss francs.

- Then there's Zimbabwe: when Zimbabwe's economy collapsed in 2009 and the currency tanked, citizens used talk time minutes as an alternative currency.

- And the town of Brixton, in the United Kingdom, uses their own currency—called Brixton pounds—for local trade, to encourage people to maintain and build their local community. It's true. You can go into shops and use Brixton pounds; the local shopkeepers are then able to use them to buy other goods and services from other local shops within Brixton.

OK, remember that trivia question we asked you: what is the one alternative currency you loved, especially as a child? We think it's time to answer it, just in case you haven't guessed.

That's right. The answer is brownie points (at least in the United States)! In other countries it may be gold stars or even red flowers. The point is that every culture has some sort of reward system for children.

Brownie points are just one method of rewarding children for their achievements and allowing them to exchange these points for something of value. Children earn brownie points for completing tasks or doing something good—it's one of the oldest and most basic exchange systems around. Children can cash in their points for something they want: "Mom, I did the dishes, can I go watch television for an hour?"

Are we saying that cryptocurrency is just like brownie points; you can exchange it for an extra hour of television? Well, not exactly—although it's not far off.

Which leads us to the next question, and the first one people ask us at cocktail parties when they find out we run a cryptocurrency podcast and YouTube show called *The Coin Chat.*

WHAT IS A CRYPTOCURRENCY?

The easiest way to explain it is to tell you what cryptocurrency is *not*. It's not dollars, or yen, or rupees, or euros, or any of the national currencies with which we're all familiar. These are known as fiat currencies, meaning they're government-regulated and government-backed. There's general agreement about how they're valued, traded, and issued.

If you think about it, you often refer to currency as what you spend. For example, the national currency in Great Britain is British pounds; you spend pounds, which you also call quid. In the United States, you have dollars and spend dollars or bucks.

WHAT IS FIAT CURRENCY?
(NOT TO BE CONFUSED WITH THE ITALIAN CAR!)

The term "fiat" comes from Latin, meaning "Let it be done;" used as an order or decree.

Fiat money is any currency that is often backed by governments and their regulations. The value of the currency is established by the government and becomes legal tender which we all recognize as having a certain value that enables us to buy and sell things within the country.

So why are we telling you this?

Because we talk about cryptocurrency in a similar way to how we refer to fiat currencies. The units of money in cryptocurrency are called coins. Bitcoin is one of many types of cryptocurrencies. The smallest unit of Bitcoin is called a Satoshi.

However, unlike fiat currency (dollars, pounds, yen, etc.), which you can only spend, coins are used in a variety of ways. Coins can be used as a method of payment or as a store of value, and in some ways, they can mimic shares. Coins can also have a utility value (or a token value, which we'll get into more in the next chapter).

In other words, coins transcend what we typically think of as:

1. Currency to spend
2. Utility as a reward, fee, gift, or benefit
3. Shares in companies

Coins have the characteristics of all three at the same time.

Here are some examples of how coins can be used. You can:

- Transfer money to anyone in the world within minutes (with very low fees).

- Buy things online (airplane tickets, online shopping).

- Spend it at your local grocery store, pay your babysitter, or buy a coffee at a local café.

- Put it on a Visa or Mastercard debit card and spend it.

- Buy coins as an investment in companies and projects.

- Buy and hold coins, watching the value continue to rise as more and more people get into it.

And this is just the beginning.

THE RISE OF BITCOIN

Perhaps you've heard of Satoshi Nakamoto. He's the founder of Bitcoin. Or is he? Satoshi is the person or group that created Bitcoin, although nobody knows for sure who or what he really is. We're serious. "His" identity remains a mystery.

In October 2008, someone (or a group, nobody knows) using the name Satoshi Nakamoto published the famous white paper describing a vision for a digital currency called Bitcoin. A few months later, in 2009, Satoshi released the first specifications and proof of concept that launched Bitcoin.

That white paper of Satoshi Nakamoto turned a lot of heads because it laid out a completely new and exciting system where two people can send money to each other through a trusted network (run completely by computers), with transactions that are reliable, fast, and convenient. And you can track your transactions online, something you can't do in banking. The ease of sending and tracking a transaction was one of the first things that really appealed to people.

People started perceiving value in Bitcoin and suddenly, it wasn't just a way to send funds, it was a way to spend and invest as well. With that, Bitcoin took off. And when we say, "Bitcoin took off," it might be an understatement.

This led to the creation of cryptocurrency exchanges. When the first Bitcoin exchange was launched on March 17, 2010, one Bitcoin was worth about $0.003. Two months later, on May 22, 2010, Laszlo Hanyecz made the first Bitcoin transaction. At that time, Bitcoin was worth $0.01.

BITCOIN PIZZA

Laszlo Hanyecz, who will forever be known as the Bitcoin pizza guy, made the first recorded physical purchase with Bitcoin when he posted an offer of 10,000 Bitcoin for someone to deliver two pizzas to him. It was May 22, 2010, he was living in Florida, and 10,000 Bitcoin was worth about $40, or a couple of pizzas from Papa John's. Today, 10,000 Bitcoin is worth a lot more! (Price varies too much to give an accurate number, but it's in the millions.) That's a lot of pizza!

Once people created a demand by buying Bitcoin, the value increased. As a matter of fact, the value of Bitcoin has increased every year making it one of the most valuable currencies in the world. *Almost* more valuable than brownie points (or gold stars or red flowers).

If one Bitcoin is worth thousands of dollars, how could you possibly afford it unless you are super rich? The beauty of Bitcoin is that it can be broken down into fractions. In fact, the smallest fraction that can be sent (or purchased) is one hundred millionth of a Bitcoin. That's 0.00000001! The unit is called a Satoshi after the founder. And it makes buying Bitcoin as an investment accessible to anyone.

How much do you think one Satoshi is worth in US dollars? We're going to give you the opportunity to figure this out on your own. Of course, we'll give you a hint:

Go here to check out the current price of Bitcoin at 99Bitcoins.

www.99bitcoins.com/satoshi-usd-converter/

Okay, at this point you're probably thinking Bitcoin sounds interesting, maybe even valuable, but you wonder how it actually works. How do you spend it, buy it, send it, and invest in it? Well, those are the key questions everyone has when they first start out.

You may have noticed that sometimes Bitcoin is capitalized, and sometimes it is not.

Generally speaking, Bitcoin (with a capital "B") is used as a proper noun—when you're referencing the blockchain or project or when you're referring to the company. Whereas, bitcoin (with a lowercase "b") is used as currency—similar to "dollars."

For the sake of simplicity, however, we have chosen to capitalize Bitcoin throughout this book.

So, without further delay, let's jump right in.

CHAPTER TWO

HOW EASY IS IT TO SPEND YOUR COINS?

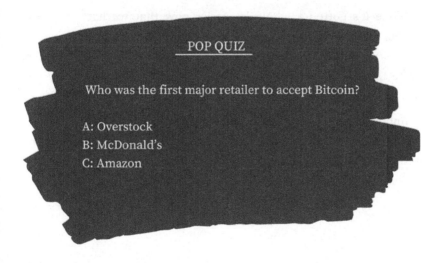

POP QUIZ

Who was the first major retailer to accept Bitcoin?

A: Overstock
B: McDonald's
C: Amazon

For about a year (from late 2016 to the end of 2017), we had a weekly experiment where we tried to spend Bitcoin in retail shops. And what did we learn? It was really hard to do.

Here's a funny thing that happened in Dubai International Airport, with a barista at a coffee shop:

Steve: "Good morning, can I get a flat white?"

Barista: "Yep, no problem."

Steve: "Can I pay with Bitcoin?"

Barista: Blink. Blink. "What do you mean, can you pay with Bitcoin?"

Steve: "You know, with Bitcoin."

Barista: "Really? I've always wanted to see a Bitcoin. Do you have one? I would love to see it! I don't know what it looks like?"

The barista honestly had no idea what Bitcoin was. He had heard of it and was curious, but that was it. In the end, the barista accepted a Bitcoin credit card; and even though there was some confusion about whether their system could handle it, it worked just fine.

While it's gotten a whole lot easier now that we have a growing number of cryptocurrency debit cards and people are starting to accept coins as a payment in their shops, most people still won't know what you're talking about when you mention Bitcoin. If they do, they don't have the facilities to accept cryptocurrencies yet. But that's all changing.

And since coins are used as currency, utility, and as shares, you can spend them in three very different ways. So, let's look briefly at each of these uses so that you understand how coins work and why they are so diverse and interesting.

CURRENCY: HOW TO SPEND YOUR COINS

For the moment, let's assume you've already purchased some Bitcoin.

BRISBANE AIRPORT

In 2018, the Brisbane International Airport became the world's first crypto-friendly airport. They now allow you to use Bitcoin (and other cryptocurrencies) at the various shopping and dining facilities throughout their terminals. This is no small feat considering Brisbane is the third-largest airport in the country, but in May of 2018, the Brisbane Airport Corporations announced their partnership with the Australian payment provider Travelbybit.

There are many companies that accept Bitcoin, and sometimes a variety of other cryptocurrencies. Software company ProfitTrailer, for example, lets you pay in Bitcoin to subscribe to their online trading software. You can pay for products on Amazon using the Moon browser extension (paywithmoon.com). And you can spend your cryptocurrency using Spedn (spedn.io) on your smartphone on Android and Apple. In fact, there are many companies now starting to accept digital payments with cryptocurrency, including Expedia, Overstock, and Microsoft Xbox. There's even a coffee shop in Prague that only accepts Bitcoin and Litecoin (we'll get to Litecoin and other forms of cryptocurrency soon). And the list grows by the day!

Back in 2011, I launched a bottled water company called IndigoH2O, which won three international awards and was the third most popular premium brand. Riding on my success at the time, I decided to run a marketing stunt— I would accept Bitcoin, making us the first water company in the world to do so. While I got a lot of press and marketing attention, I didn't manage to sell any bottles for Bitcoin. The funny thing is, I didn't really understand Bitcoin and just did it for publicity. I wish I had actually known more and bought some Bitcoin at the time.

MORE WAYS TO SPEND YOUR BITCOIN

*CoinMap - A list of 900 Bitcoin friendly businesses & ATMs

*Lolli - Earn free bitcoin when you shop online

*Virgin Galactic - You can pay in Bitcoin

*Microsoft - Buy games, movies, or apps on Windows or XBox Stores

*CheapAir & Expedia - Pay for flights and book hotels using Bitcoin

*DISH Network - Has been accepting Bitcoin since 2014

One of the easiest ways to spend your cryptocurrency is to get a cryptocurrency debit card. There are a few options out there and the list continues to grow. Some of the more notable vendors include BitPay, Wirex, and Change. These vendors issue you a Visa or Mastercard debit card so you can buy things online and in shops. All you have to do is send your Bitcoin or other accepted coins straight to the card. You'll have those funds within minutes and then you can start spending them right away.

It really is that simple!

Lots of people are amazed to think using cryptocurrency could be this easy, but there's no reason for it to be hard. Like any technology, it always starts out very techie and gets easier to use over time. Every technology has gone from complicated to easy, enabling adoption to go mainstream. Cryptocurrency is no exception.

TOKENS: ANOTHER WAY TO SPEND COINS AS A UTILITY

Do you have loyalty or rewards cards from your favorite shops, or a cashback rewards credit card?

You can think of tokens as reward points when you're working with cryptocurrency. They're still coins, but since they're being used as a utility, we often call them tokens (honestly, it does tend to confuse things at times, but we just want to make you aware).

Tokens are earned from a specific company or project (we'll talk about projects soon) much the way you earn reward or loyalty points. For both tokens and loyalty points, you use them in the shop where you earned them or redeem them for discounts. The difference: you don't need to fill your pocket full of loyalty cards because all your tokens (coins) can be stored in an exciting electronic wallet.

Still a little confused? Don't worry. The important thing to understand right now: tokens are the same as coins. They're just being used as a utility.

COINS AS AN INVESTMENT LIKE SHARES

The third way coins are used is like shares—an investment into new cryptocurrency companies and projects. We're going to expand on this a lot more, but for now we just want to give you an overview of this concept.

Normally, when you invest, you use your currency to buy shares. But coins are both used as currency and traded as shares. So, if there's a coin you're really interested in, you can invest in that coin the way you would invest in Microsoft, by buying its shares. However, while you could never buy a coffee with Microsoft shares, you could use your invested coins to buy a coffee.

POP QUIZ ANSWER

Remember our trivia question:
Who was the first major retailer to accept Bitcoin?

ANSWER: Overstock. CEO Patrick Byrne was a big proponent of Bitcoin back in 2014. Overstock continues to look for new and innovative ways to utilize the blockchain. If you guessed McDonald's, there were unconfirmed rumours they would accept Bitcoin. We are still waiting to buy a Happy Meal.

CHAPTER THREE

WHAT THE HECK IS A BLOCKCHAIN?

B efore we jump into blockchain (what it is and how it works), we've got a trivia question for you:

What's another technology that was difficult for people to wrap their heads around when it was first developed?

We'll give you the answer to this one right now because we see some remarkable similarities to how blockchain and cryptocurrency have started and are progressing their way into the mainstream.

The answer: the Internet.

When the Internet first came out, it was very technical and people couldn't understand what it was, how it worked, or why they would even want to use it. It seemed scary, uncomfortable, and was very hard to understand. In fact, many people thought it was a fad that would simply fade away.

On February 27, 1995, Newsweek shared the "truth" about the Internet:

"The truth is no online database will replace your daily newspaper, no CD-ROM can take the place of a competent teacher, and no computer network will change the way government works," wrote Clifford Stoll, "How about electronic publishing? Try reading a book on disc. Yet Nicholas Negroponte, director of the MIT Media Lab, predicts that we'll soon buy books and newspapers straight over the Internet. Uh, sure"

Seventeen years later, Newsweek ceased print publication and became exclusively available online.

As we all know, the Internet wasn't a fad, it was just misunderstood when it first started. It progressed and developed over time.

The first wave of the Internet was created by the United States government and called ARPANET (from the US Advanced Research Projects Agency, which goes all the way back to 1967). It was used as a system for the military to communicate between departments. Eventually, it was spun out to become Internet 1.0, the first stage of the Internet. Do you remember Gopher and printing search results out on your dot matrix printer?

Internet 2.0 was more about collaboration, stimulated by the transition to mobile apps, social media, and smartphones. While this technology has made our lives easier, it's also led to a variety of data breaches and the loss of our privacy due to trusting large companies to safeguard our personal information. (You probably never imagined that providing random information or using your smartphone would lead to the levels of targeted marketing that you experience today.)

So, what's the link between the Internet history and blockchain?

Internet 3.0 is a new evolving paradigm where blockchain is using the Internet infrastructure to give us a much faster, more secure environment. With the blockchain, you can regain control of your privacy while gaining access to a variety of new services without feeling your data is beyond your own control. We're telling you this because it's changing quickly, and we don't want you to be left behind.

To understand how all this change is possible, let's look at what enables a blockchain to protect our privacy, create applications, and create new currencies. Then we can take a closer look at the different types of coins that are created as result of these various blockchains.

THE ABCS OF BLOCKCHAIN

It's true what they say: a picture is worth a thousand words. That's why we're going to start by defining blockchain with this graphic:

 WHAT IS A BLOCKCHAIN?

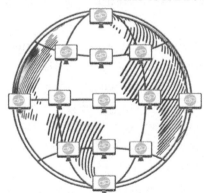

- A blockchain is a chain of blocks
- Each block is a confirmation of a transaction
- Multiple confirmations (blocks) are required to confirm your transaction
- Once a minimum number of confirmations is reached your funds are released
- Each block/confirmation forms a chain of blocks and hence the name blockchain

A blockchain can also be described by its few unique features and functions:

- A blockchain is like an operating system.

- Each public blockchain creates a unique cryptocurrency and each cryptocurrency has coins we can send, buy, spend, and invest.

- Each blockchain has a ledger that stores and records all transactions.

To help give you a better picture of a blockchain, we'll expand upon each of these features and functions by comparing it to something you're already familiar with. Before you know it, you'll have a clearer image in your head.

A BLOCKCHAIN IS AN OPERATING SYSTEM

Think of your PC or smartphone. They run on Microsoft Windows, Google Android, or Mac Operating Systems. These core operating systems allow your devices to work. The same might be said about a blockchain. Each blockchain has its own unique way of working (similar to Mac versus Windows) offering different features, usability, speed, privacy, and functions you may or may not use.

With an operating system, you can build applications that run on it. When you think about applications that run on your Mac or PC or smartphone, you've got apps such as McAfee Antivirus software, Microsoft Office Suite, or that really awesome game you love playing. You may even have a YouTube app on your smartphone where you can watch super content about cryptocurrency, such as *The Coin Chat* (shameless plug, but hopefully you get the idea).

In much the same way, you can build apps that run on the blockchain. We refer to these apps as DApps or decentralized apps. Unlike an operating system like Mac or Windows, the blockchain is fully decentralized; it's not controlled by anyone and it's not stored centrally. Each blockchain is created and deployed around the world across multiple computers so everyone can access and use it together. Yes, we know this is a bit of a foreign concept, but we want to make sure you understand the basics.

The benefit of a decentralized application is that it can't be censored by a central body or organization; no central authority can revoke your transactions or delay it like a bank can. There's also the added convenience of being able to send funds quickly without intermediaries and with privacy intact.

You also gain control over your own data. It's not stored by the product or service you're using (unlike Facebook, which has had a variety of issues with data protection and data privacy starting with the Cambridge Analytica scandal). If you use a competitive blockchain project such as Minds.com, a decentralized alternative to Facebook, they have no access to or control of your data.

That being said, a blockchain isn't just an operating system. It's a whole lot more.

EVERY PUBLIC BLOCKCHAIN CREATES A CRYPTOCURRENCY (AND COINS)

Yes, you read that correctly. Every time a new public blockchain is created, a new cryptocurrency is created, too. As we mentioned at the start of the book, a cryptocurrency is the currency and the coins are what you spend (plus it has the added benefit of being used as a utility and can be traded like shares). Just remember: each fiat currency is money like US dollars or British pounds. You spend the dollars and pounds (or bucks and quid). And each cryptocurrency has a form of money you can spend called coins.

Unfortunately, we tend to make things a bit confusing in the world of cryptocurrency. As a rule, we just refer to the blockchain, cryptocurrency, and coin by the coin name just to make conversations a whole lot easier. For example, when we talk about Bitcoin, we're talking about the specific coin, the cryptocurrency, and the blockchain all at once.

Now that you understand that each new public blockchain creates a new cryptocurrency and associated coin, let's look at how the blockchain is used to enable you to send your coins to each other with the blockchain recording each transaction that takes place.

STORING TRANSACTIONS ON A LEDGER, BLOCK BY BLOCK

Think of a blockchain like an online ledger that an accountant uses to keep track of all business transactions. The blockchain automatically documents every single cryptocurrency transaction.

Anytime somebody buys, sells, or sends coins, those transactions are recorded in a public ledger. The transactions do not expose any of your personal information—they're public, but your personal information is not. (We'll get into this in a lot more detail when we talk about coins and wallets. For now, just rest assured that your personal information is still secure and not available to prying eyes.)

The thing that's different about this ledger, the blockchain ledger, is that it contains millions and millions of transactions which are continuously being recorded and sent to hundreds of thousands of computers all over the world to verify and confirm the transactions.

VERIFYING THE TRANSACTIONS (MINING)

When you send Bitcoin (or any coin) to a friend, the transaction isn't instantaneous. Oh, we may have inadvertently led you to believe it is, but in truth, the transaction takes anywhere from a few seconds up to an hour to go through the verification process. But unlike a bank, the cryptocurrency world runs twenty-four hours a day, seven days a week, and that verification process begins right away.

Transactions are processed by a network of computers set up and connected to the Bitcoin blockchain. The computers serve the same role as bankers verifying transactions.

This network of computers works together to cross-reference and verify each transaction. In other words, the computers must agree with each other; when one computer doesn't agree with the others, that computer is tossed out of the network for generating incorrect results.

For each transaction, the funds must be verified several times before they're confirmed. Each confirmation is called a block (or block confirmation). The sequence of blocks being confirmed one after the other creates a chain of blocks (hence, the name). We refer to this as the confirmation process.

For a transaction to complete, a minimum number of confirmations are required—normally, a minimum of three. We refer to this as consensus, the process of having multiple computers verify and confirm a transaction to ensure it is handled correctly and safely, every time, without error.

The bad transactions are weeded out while the verified transactions are permanently stored on the blockchain (in the ledger).

Wait, we know what you're thinking. At least we think we do: there has to be an intermediary to process and verify these transactions, right? When comparing to the banking process, you may hear us say blockchain transactions occur without an intermediary, but it's slightly more complicated than that.

The individuals that provide and maintain the massive network of computers all over the world are called miners. The miners' role is simply to provide the equipment needed to verify transactions. Miners are rewarded with "block rewards" and some fees from transactions for their efforts to supply computer equipment, electricity, and equipment maintenance.

What's a block reward? Block rewards are new coins that get mined (created) over time. Here's how it works: when you send money to a friend, newly mined coins are distributed automatically as a payment to the miners for providing their computers to verify the transaction. (We'll explain this a bit further when we talk about "halvenings" later.)

So, what's a bad transaction? (And you thought we were going to leave you hanging . . .) Normally, a bad transaction is caused by a nefarious actor who wishes to disrupt a transaction for personal gain. This, of course is not in the interest of anyone who wants to have a safe and trusted network. The confirmation process is designed to ensure that any outliers are immediately identified and stopped.

Having multiple confirmations ensures that no single computer is singlehandedly responsible for any single transaction. This creates an incredibly stable and safe environment for you to make a transaction.

A PUBLIC BUT NOT SO PUBLIC LEDGER

Your funds are recorded on the ledger in wallet addresses, which are only known to you. This means only you truly know what you have. (Hang on to that thought, we'll dive into "wallets" soon.)

So, while the transactions are being stored in a public ledger, nobody is sharing your personal information. And if you're worried about having your transactions available for the world to see like your latest Mastercard statement, there are privacy coins, too. We'll get into those in the next chapter.

The beauty of the blockchain is that you can't go back and change what's already been documented on the public ledger. It would mean changing a backdated block within a chain of blocks that's already been written and confirmed—and that's not possible. Unlike a company ledger (where changes can be made on past or present data), the blockchain ledger is tamper-proof and written electronically, one block at a time, so it's next to impossible to modify previously confirmed blocks.

Why would someone want to change something on the public ledger?

Let's say you wanted to buy a motorcycle from your neighbor for three Bitcoin. It's a simple transaction: once they deliver the bike, you transfer three Bitcoin. However, if you actually managed to do the nearly impossible and hacked into a blockchain (performing a 51% attack, meaning you have overpowered the voting rights of the network), you could reverse the transaction on the blockchain, and have all of your coins refunded. In the end, you would be the owner of a new motorcycle as well as the three Bitcoin you used to buy it. Nice for you, but not so nice for your neighbor.

But in the blockchain, once the transaction is transmitted, it's stored and unchangeable. As you make further transactions like selling the motorcycle, the newest data (owner and price) could also be stored on the blockchain. You always have the full history of data for every transaction, and none of it can be tampered with. This creates a far safer and more trusted way to store the history of a transaction.

If a blockchain is comprised of hundreds of computers, you may be wondering how it can really be safe. After all, there are any number of ways to tamper with a computer; and we all know hackers are getting more sophisticated.

Well, here's how blockchains protect you:

Blockchains run on a set of complex cryptographic algorithms, which makes them pretty hard to crack—certainly harder than hacking most anything else out there. And because there are so many computers running all around the world, short of a global power outage, there is no way to actually shutdown a blockchain. So, the combination of a vast array of computers all running with extreme encryption using complex algorithms makes for a very safe and secure environment.

Now that you've got the basics of what a blockchain is, let's talk about cryptocurrency and the different types of coins you might encounter and want to use.

CHAPTER FOUR

A COIN IS JUST A COIN, OR IS IT?

C oins are unique. We've covered how they represent value as a currency, have a utility function, and are also used like shares, as an investment. However, not all coins work in the same way. There are four different types of coins, each with their own characteristics:

- Coins as currency, or a store of value
- Coins that are created by companies or projects
- Stable coins
- Coins that are digital collectible items

So, let's dig in a bit further, coin by coin, so this all makes "cents."

COINS AS CURRENCY

You can think of these coins as a store of value—they're used to buy something, or they're stored, like gold, for long-term value. In addition, there are two types of currency coins: public coins, such as Bitcoin, and privacy coins.

PUBLIC COINS

Bitcoin is the most common public coin and certainly the easiest to understand. You can spend and earn Bitcoin—much like any other currency—and you can also invest in it. What makes this coin public is the fact that the ledgers and all transactions within the Bitcoin blockchain can be openly viewed online.

Sending and receiving coins requires having a wallet address (which we'll get to in the next chapter). A wallet address is composed of unique letters and numbers only known to you. Remember, although we call them public, none of your personal data is exposed online anywhere. The only information shown involves the actual transaction—the movement of the coins from one wallet to another. We'll cover this in more detail when we discuss wallets and sending coins, so keep reading.

PRIVACY COINS

As you can imagine, you may not want all your transactions and coins on display for the world to see (much the way you wouldn't want your neighbors to know how much money you have and where you're spending it). That's where privacy coins come in.

In traditional banking, your bank account is yours and it's private; only you (and the bank manager) know what's in it. With privacy coins, your coins are yours and they're private. If you spend them, only you know where they're spent (and, of course, the person or place that receives them). The difference: with privacy coins, you're in full control of your coins and no one else can see what you have . . . ever.

Examples of privacy coins include DASH, Monero, Horizen, Zcash, Grin, and AmityCoin, just to name a few. They still represent value; you just get to keep them private, similar to having your funds in a bank account. Pretty simple, right?

COINS THAT ARE PROJECTS (ALTCOINS)

We're used to thinking of money as something earned, spent, or saved; stocks and bonds are separate, only for investing. We're asking you to forget what you currently know about money and shares, so we can show you the paradigm shift that has occurred and how it works.

It starts with the coins created by companies or projects.

They create what are known as Alternative Coins (Altcoins). Since we're not necessarily talking about companies (you'll see what we mean in a minute), for the rest of the book we'll simply refer to Altcoins as projects.

Typically, project coins are created by groups of people building something they believe has value to others. These groups of people might be a registered company, they might be part of a foundation, or they might be a group of volunteers who contribute to an open source project interested in future income and having an impact on the world.

Here's where we get into that paradigm shift—open source projects are a way that people can work together to create unique software. These projects consist of volunteers who contribute to the development of the software and the blockchain, without any compensation. Yes, we know receiving no compensation for your work sounds odd, but it's not as far-fetched as you might think.

Here's an interesting example: chances are good you've heard of (or even seen) a "flash mob." It's an organized group that suddenly shows up somewhere, does some sort of coordinated performance (music, song, or dance), then fades back into the crowd. They don't work for anyone; they do it because they love performing; it's a fantastic stunt; it makes people happy; it's fun.

In fact, there are a lot of volunteer and charity organizations out there, too. Many people are willing to provide their time to help a cause bigger than themselves.

Projects are no different. In blockchain, many of the projects are developed by a group of volunteers working together toward a single goal to create something amazing. They create a blockchain and a coin that can be used within their application so others can benefit from and use their DApp. In exchange for their time and efforts, they often earn some of their coins as a reward for their contribution.

And there are a lot of Altcoins.

Since Bitcoin made its debut in 2009, there's been an explosion of Altcoins. It didn't take long for people to realize they could build a whole variety of new blockchains and cryptocurrencies (with new coins, of course).

The crazy thing is anyone can make a coin. Yup, you read that correctly. But remember, cryptocurrency coins are digital and not physical. And coins really should have some form of utility value, some way to use them, if they're worth creating. Sure, there are people out there creating coins just to scam people, but the vast majority of coins are really adding value, which you'll see as you read on.

The most notable of the Altcoins is Ethereum. Their team have built a blockchain to serve as an operating system to enable other smaller projects to launch their projects on top. Ethereum has its own coin called Ether or ETH. Many projects may not have the funds to build their own blockchain initially, so they build their DApp, create their own coin, and use an operating system blockchain such as Ethereum to get up and running a whole lot faster. Eventually these projects may create their own blockchain so that they can build all of the features and services that they want which may not be available from an operating system project such as Ethereum.

So, why would you purchase or invest in such coins? Because when these open source projects succeed, their coins can dramatically rise in value. Suddenly their achievements are recognized; their product or solution is seen to deliver real world value. It doesn't always happen, but when it does, enjoy the run up.

COINS THAT ARE TIED TO FIAT (STABLE COINS)

Stable coins work just like US dollars (USD) except they're cryptocurrency coins instead.

Unlike currency coins, which fluctuate in price all the time, stable coins are tied to a fiat currency (such as the USD), so they're always valued at one dollar, for example.

Stable coins are all backed by companies or governments that have dollars to enable the coins to be stable. Some of the notable ones are USD Tether (USDT), Circle USD Coin (USDC), and Gemini USD (GUSD).

The real value of stable coins is their ability to be tethered to a stable currency. So, when coins like Bitcoin are fluctuating a lot, you might want to store your money in a stable coin instead to avoid volatility.

Spending stable coins like fiat will certainly evolve and become more mainstream at some point. However, at the time of writing this book, you can't spend the stable coins but we're sure the ability to do so isn't far off.

On the plus side, you can hold your money so it's stable. This is especially useful when the markets get volatile and you don't want to risk losing what you already have. It's also great when you want to trade Bitcoin to USD and don't want to get hit with all those high banking fees.

This advice will honestly save you a bundle. We wish someone had told us this from the start to reduce all of our costs. We'll talk about all of this in more detail when we talk about trading.

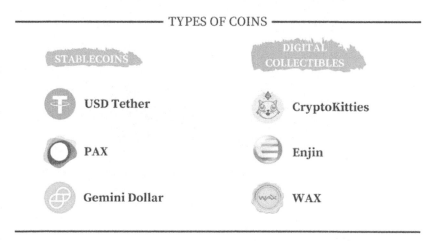

———————————— TYPES OF COINS ————————————

STABLECOINS

USD Tether

PAX

Gemini Dollar

DIGITAL COLLECTIBLES

CryptoKitties

Enjin

WAX

COINS THAT ARE DIGITAL COLLECTIBLE ITEMS

Now, here's an interesting type of coin that might take you totally by surprise. They're collectible coins, and they're completely unique—no two coins are the same.

Remember when kids used to collect and trade baseball cards back in the day, or Pokémon cards more recently? Digital collectible coins draw interest and investment in much the same way. Unlike collectible cards, which produced multiple copies of rare cards, each collectible coin is unlike any other one in the world. They're considered collectible items and may go up in value. If you can get your hands on the right coin, you could stand to make a lot of money.

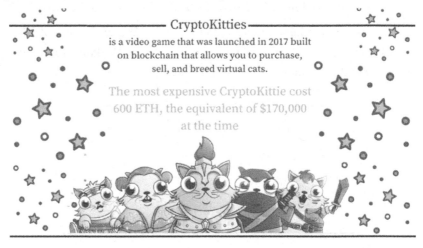

CryptoKitties

is a video game that was launched in 2017 built on blockchain that allows you to purchase, sell, and breed virtual cats.

The most expensive CryptoKittie cost 600 ETH, the equivalent of $170,000 at the time

CryptoKitties is a good example: a blockchain game launched in 2017, it allows you to purchase, sell, and breed virtual cats.

No, we did not make that up.

In CryptoKitties, your goal is to collect and breed cats to ultimately grow your litter. Once you start breeding your kitties, you can create entirely new breeds with a variety of characteristics. Each cat can have its own value, because each CryptoKitty is unique.

And if you're lucky, you can make some money in the process. But, it's not all fun and games and kitty litter. You'll need to spend some of your own coins to buy cats and improve them.

Sounds silly right? Well, it was a massive hit. At one point it was so popular that CryptoKitty transactions completely clogged the Ethereum blockchain.

THE FUTURE OF COINS

There are a couple of things coins do that maybe you haven't heard of before. The following concepts, if understood, could potentially increase the value of any investment you choose to make.

The two profit-boosting topics we'll cover are forks and halvenings. Let's look at what they are, how they play out in the crypto world, and what you might expect in the future when traditional companies start embracing blockchain technology and cryptocurrency.

SOFT AND HARD FORKS

Before cracking open this book, you had most likely heard of Bitcoin— but what about Ethereum; how about Ripple, Litecoin, Monero, or Zcash. Had you heard of Bitcoin spinoffs including (but definitely not limited to) Bitcoin Cash (now Bitcoin Cash ABC and Bitcoin Cash SV), Bitcoin Diamond, Bitcoin Unlimited, Bitcoin Gold, and Bitcoin Platinum?

We're guessing probably not, and the list of coins and their spinoffs is actually a lot bigger. In fact, a spinoff is where a project splits into two separate projects. There have been several projects that split into two, and there will certainly be more in the future.

And those spinoffs have a name: forks. Just bear with us a second while we explain this; then you'll see why it's so important to know what a fork is and how you might stand to make more money as a result.

In most cases, a fork is nothing more than a software upgrade of a blockchain and its associated coin (often referred to as a soft fork). For the upgrade to go forward smoothly, it requires everyone involved in the maintenance and support of the coin and its blockchain to agree that such a change would be advantageous or necessary. Generally, there are two major groups that must agree: the developers who write the blockchain software, and the miners who verify transactions. On occasion, there is disagreement between developers and/or miners and that leads to what we call a hard fork.

If a hard fork happens, the original coin in question will be split into two unique blockchains—in other words, two different coins, managed by two separate teams. The original coin is effectively turned into two different projects as each team goes a different direction. You get both coins, and your total investment could potentially increase in value.

This, of course, is a very simplified explanation of how soft and hard forks work, but it's enough to give you the benefits of any future "spinoffs," to get extra coins and future value. If you'd care to learn more about soft and hard forks, check out some of our additional content on our website here:

www.beleftbehind.com/bonus-content.

LITECOIN: THE FIRST BITCOIN SPINOFF?

Unlike other types of forks, Litecoin was created by taking the original Bitcoin core development team to launch a new coin in 2011 - more of a "spinoff fork" than a soft fork or hard fork.

So what makes it different? Well, their founder, Charlie Lee, made changes to the code to make it faster for transactions and increased the total number of coins, amongst other things.

HALVENING (SOMETHING UNIQUE THAT MAY DRIVE YOUR COIN PRICE UP)

Halvening is a topic that frequently comes up when we discuss cryptocurrency; it's understandable—it can have a significant effect on your account value over the long term.

It started when some of the major coins like Bitcoin, Litecoin, and Ethereum were created, they designed a model where the number of coins rewarded to miners reduces over time.

Here's how it works:

Bitcoin has a total supply of 21 million coins that will be slowly released (mined) over time. The process of mining is what releases the coins into circulation. Not all coins are available today; roughly 82% of the total number of coins have already been mined and are in circulation already—the remainder are held in an electronic reserve and will be slowly released over time. Approximately every four years, the number of Bitcoin "mined" is reduced, or halved.

With an increasing number of people, like you, getting into Bitcoin, the total number of transactions continues to rise, giving miners slightly more in transaction fees while their block rewards are being reduced. This ensures miners continue to get rewarded for their efforts to confirm the transactions on the blockchain network. Since the supply of Bitcoin is limited, as the demand continues to increase, so will the price of Bitcoin, otherwise known as scarcity.

This halvening process will run until all 21 million Bitcoin have been "mined" and released to the public. As a result, we expect the price of Bitcoin will continue to go through additional four-year cycles, where the price will rise as each halvening occurs, and then stabilize until the next period.

More adoption means more people, even companies, getting involved with blockchain. These changes have already started taking place and will continue as more major companies use blockchain to change the way they do business. And to learn even more about passive income in cryptocurrency, you can check out our website: www.beleftbehind.com/bonus-content.

BIG CORPORATIONS AND CRYPTOCURRENCY

If you want to know how fast cryptocurrency is moving, consider this: when we first wrote this section in March of 2019, Facebook had yet to announce their Libra coin.

The next successful coin might not come from a startup at all. It could be a traditional tech company, like Google, or maybe a company like Facebook or Netflix. We're curious to see exactly how it all plays out, but it's just a matter of time before one of the big names enters this space. In fact, Amazon bought a few URLs:

- amazonbitcoin.com
- amazonetherum.com
- amazoncryptocurrency.com
- amazoncryptocurrencies.com

Who knows what will come next.

In a nutshell, the Libra project will create a global stable coin that will enable everyone who uses Facebook to use the coin to pay for advertising, as well as transact with each other globally. It will store all transactions on a global blockchain ledger and create a new way for people around the world to gain access to cryptocurrency without it being technical or complicated.

Just watch as more of the big-name companies attempt to transition into the world of blockchain and cryptocurrency.

CHAPTER FIVE

WHAT IS A WALLET AND A WALLET ADDRESS?

I n banking, you have a bank account with an account number. In cryptocurrency, you have a wallet with a wallet address.

When someone refers to sending or storing coins in their wallet, they really mean their wallet address. The coins are just records stored on the blockchain; your wallet shows the balance. This is important because it's the foundation for how you send, receive, store, and invest your coins.

Here are some examples of what wallet addresses look like (these are the addresses we use for our "tip jar" on our show—you're more than welcome to show us some love too).

─────────────── TIP JAR ───────────────

Bitcoin:	1Bs6JckqCECWXvCVAUJN9mFKebVwsxgteH
Bitcoin Cash:	qp4la9efsxpukt80q6whkv3gymz6v6g3wqf58rw2v3
Ethereum:	0xa69160c7dC2F66b0b309AC3D27565fE69C06904E
Litecoin:	LQ5HZundFbLhLGVKoqFEjzwAAFzrWxGEta
ZCash:	t1cNeraRUNDc9D9FBo8xCaqzb79eK3UB2bv

Notice how different coins have different wallet address formats. Ethereum, for example, always starts with "0x." Every coin has a unique format and different length of characters. No two coins are the same although some may look very similar so be aware that when you send your funds you send them to the correct address and format.

Now here's where things get interesting. If you have several different types of coins, each coin is stored in a different wallet address. It's the same as placing different fiat currencies (dollars and euros, for example) into different account numbers in your bank. Each account number holds a different currency—each wallet address stores a different coin. Naturally, just as you can have multiple account numbers in your bank for the same currency, you can have multiple wallet addresses for the same type of coin. You can have three Bitcoin in one wallet (address), and six Bitcoin in another.

TYPES OF WALLETS

And there are three types of wallets: software wallets, hardware wallets, and paper wallets.

Types of Cryptocurrency Wallets

	Online	Safe	Economical
Software Wallets Software that you download to your PC	✓	✕	✓
Hardware Wallets It's an actual device that looks like a USB that allows you to store your coins offline	✕	✓	✕
Paper Wallets Piece of paper that has your private key written on it	✕	✓	✓

SOFTWARE WALLETS

A software wallet is exactly what it sounds like—software you download onto your PC or smartphone.

If you go to CryptoCompare.com/wallets you'll see a list of software wallets. They have a whole series of wallets and software packages. It's just a matter of finding the one that has the coins you want to hold. If you have Bitcoin, Litecoin, and Ethereum, then you need to make sure that the software wallet supports all three types of coins. You may have to download several different wallets when you start getting more advanced. Each wallet will have a unique wallet address for each coin. Think of each wallet address as a bank account. Normally you just have a single currency account. But if you have multiple currencies in your bank, then each account will be a different currency. Each coin that you hold is a different currency, so you need a different wallet address for each one.

Sites like CryptoCompare.com explain which coins are supported in each wallet, making it easy to choose. Two of the more popular software wallets are Exodus and Jaxx Liberty. Once you download their software, you can transfer and access your coins there.

After you install the software on your PC or smartphone, you'll be given some backup information that you need to save called a mnemonic phrase and a private key. These are the "keys" to open and secure your wallet. We'll cover this in detail in the next chapter.

HARDWARE WALLETS

A hardware wallet is an actual device that looks like a USB flash drive. It's a type of hardware device with firmware; you plug it into your PC (in the USB port) and it allows you to access your coins offline. Once plugged in, you can connect to the blockchain to synchronize your wallet with the ledger and send or receive coins. They aren't foolproof, but unless you picked up your wallet at a swap meet or from a dubious seller on an online marketplace, the odds are really low that your hardware wallet will be vulnerable to a hack.

Hardware wallets are made for only one purpose: to keep your coins safe and secure. Of course, using an offline wallet makes it more difficult to send, trade, buy, or sell. We suggest only using hardware wallets in an online mode when you are in a safe environment, like your own home network. And much like software wallets, when you first setup your hardware wallet you'll be provided with a mnemonic phrase and private key.

BUYING A HARDWARE WALLET

Some of the most popular hardware wallets are Trezor, KeepKey, Ballet, BitBox, Cryptosteel, and Ledger. These are hardware wallet companies—and we recommend buying them online, directly from the company website. We've got a list of them here so you can check them out: www.beleftbehind.com/bonus-content/.

Oh, and if anyone's paying attention: we keep waiting for someone to make a hardware wallet that looks like a little piggy bank.

UPDATING YOUR HARDWARE WALLET

Recently, Ledger issued a firmware update on the Ledger Nano S to address possible weaknesses. The standard firmware update process for most hardware wallets will verify the firmware you're downloading is from a valid source. It's kind of like downloading an update to your PC, Mac, or smartphone—you don't have to worry about it. If you install the software you get from a hardware wallet provider, you'll have several opportunities to verify the installation and connection to the hardware wallet. Don't bypass the safety checks and you're in good hands.

Now, are there any limits to the average hardware wallet or a restriction on a particular coin or combinations of coins? Theoretically, there's no limit on what coins can be backed up by hardware wallets. In practice, the value of a given hardware wallet comes down to the strength of the company's software support, what coins you can store, and any additional features.

Not to get all *Mission Impossible* on you, but some hardware wallets have a "duress" feature you can use in an emergency. In the unlikely event someone holds you at gun or knife point and tells you to unlock your hardware wallet, you would use this feature to avoid revealing the true value of the coins you hold. When you plug it into the computer and enter your duress password, it will show a fraction of your actual coin holdings. *Sorry thief, there's only $123 in here, see?* No need to reveal that your *other* password lets you access all your holdings. Let them get away with the duress coins.

This is not really a new concept; people often use decoy wallets when traveling. You might carry one wallet with all your credit cards, medical information, and driver's license in it, and another with just a small amount of cash and some expired cards. If you get held up, you can give up the duress wallet without losing everything.

PAPER WALLETS

A paper wallet is the simplest and safest of them all. It's the term used to describe the backup of your wallet addresses, including the process of documenting your passwords, mnemonic phrases, and private keys, to access those wallets. (We'll cover these new terms in the next chapter so hold tight.) For many, their paper wallet consists of a sheet of paper with the listed passwords hidden away in a safe or stored somewhere for safekeeping.

You can always receive the coins, since the sender only needs your wallet address, as a record of the coins is stored on the public ledger. So, the paper wallet is really your backup to access your coins. It can always be imported into a hardware or software wallet later (using your mnemonic phrase or private keys, coming up shortly).

Think of the paper wallet as extreme cold storage. If you don't want to spend or even touch your coins—you just want to save or hold them—the safest way to go about doing that is by backing up your wallet address details on a paper wallet, because it can't be hacked.

VIEWING YOUR WALLET ADDRESS ON THE PUBLIC LEDGER

You can check the balance of your wallet address and all of transactions by viewing them on a blockchain explorer. Popular coins like Bitcoin have a few websites you can use to check your balance. In simple terms, the explorers show you the Sender and Receiver wallet addresses for each transaction, along with the amount that was sent. They all look a bit techie, unfortunately, but are in fact really straightforward. Just remember, for privacy coins you can't see anyone's transactions online.

If you want to find a blockchain explorer, just head over to Google and search "Bitcoin explorer" or "Etherscan" (for Ether), for example.

BEING YOUR OWN BANK (THE GOOD AND THE BAD)

You trust banks to hold your money for you—that's probably why you deposited your money there in the first place. Since banks are often insured and may be backed by the government, there's always some form of reassurance your funds are safe. If the bank collapses or gets hacked, you won't lose all your money. You essentially rely on the bank to provide the protection you need to access your money, save your money, store your money, and invest your money. You trust the bank to guarantee your funds are always safe.

Except, sometimes the banks are a little too good at keeping your funds safe from you:

—————————— NORTHERN ROCK UK ——————————

When Northern Rock in the UK shut down in 2008, people were left standing in line for days to get access to their money—a problem you'll never face with a wallet. You will always have access to your coins 24/7. They're in your control and are your responsibility. You have no one else to rely upon to guarantee your funds' safety or access your funds.

The rule in cryptocurrency: you are your own bank. You're in control of your own money.

The good news about being in charge of your own wallet is fairly obvious: you're not depending on a bank to be open to complete new transactions since cryptocurrency works around the clock. Mining, or the process of verifying transactions, never sleeps. And as we have said, your coins are always safe and being confirmed all the time.

The bad news: you're in control of your own wallet and your funds stored within that wallet. There's no bank to protect your money (of course, there's no bank to block your accounts, withhold your payments, delay your payments, or cancel your cards—so maybe this is a good thing).

If your smartphone or PC gets hacked or you lose access to your wallet, then you are responsible for taking the appropriate measures to regain access to your funds. (Don't worry; we'll tell you how to keep your coins super safe in the next chapter.)

Let's be honest. Banking is convenient. You can withdraw your money whenever you want (as long as you're not travelling abroad and find your card not working); you can deposit your money and it will eventually show up with confidence (even though you're waiting a few days over a weekend or holiday sometimes).

But with crypto, you get the added benefit of having coins that aren't simply currency, they're investments, too. You can access and send your money to anyone, anywhere. And even though cryptocurrency is new and evolving and some of the services are not quite there yet, they're developing fast.

CHAPTER SIX

HOW DO YOU KEEP YOUR COINS SAFE?

There is one crucial thing to do in the world of cryptocurrency, and arguably it might be the most important thing to do. You must make sure to keep your coins safe.

Think about getting money from the ATM: you don't flash your cash around for everyone to see. You put your money somewhere safe. You keep it close to your body; but you still watch out for pickpockets.

It's very much the same for managing your coins. You don't want just anyone seeing your coins—you need to be aware that people will try to "pick your pocket." So, short of posting a fire-breathing dragon at the door to your cryptocurrency cave, here's what you should do to keep your coins safe.

*dragon not included

HOW TO MANAGE YOUR COINS

With the middleman (and his bureaucracy and fees) nearly eliminated, you must act as your own bank with cryptocurrency. You're the one responsible for protecting your own coins.

Here are the two ways to secure your wallet and keep your coins safe: private keys and mnemonic phrases (otherwise known as a seed phrase).

PRIVATE KEYS: All your coins are still on the public ledger, but you access them by using your own private key that is linked to your wallet address. Think of this as your key to access your super top-secret vault. It's the secret code—a very long string of numbers and letters that's next to impossible to crack because it's based on a cryptographic algorithm—that makes your wallet accessible. Don't lose your private keys! We can't emphasize enough the importance of storing your private keys in a secure place.

 Don't lose your private keys. Ever.

JAMES HOWELLS: A CAUTIONARY TALE

James, an IT consultant living in the UK, started mining Bitcoin back in 2009 on his laptop. He sold the laptop for parts on eBay but kept the hard drive with his 7,500 Bitcoin (and his private key to his wallet) in case it became valuable one day. That was smart. What wasn't very smart was how he accidentally threw the hard drive away in 2013. At one point the Bitcoin was valued at $80 million. If he only had that private key, he wouldn't be haggling with the city to dig up their landfill and sift through four years of garbage.

We were talking to a guy who had bought 50 Bitcoin with his friends back in 2014. They watched the value of those coins go up only to lose their private keys in 2017. They searched every hard disk; they searched all their files; nothing! They've lost those Bitcoin forever. Really, it's gone.

There's no way to recover your coins if you don't have your private keys.

---------- PRIVATE KEYS ----------

YOUR PRIVATE KEYS OPEN YOUR WALLET.
NEVER SHARE YOUR PRIVATE KEYS WITH ANYONE.
KEEP THEM PRIVATE & SAFE

| You send coins from your wallet address to your friend's wallet address | Coins sent from you to your friend are registered on the public ledger | Only your friend can accesses their wallet address and has full control with their PRIVATE KEYS |

Seriously, don't lose your private keys!

MNEMONIC PHRASE: When you start with any software or hardware wallet, it provides you with a backup phrase that's typically 12 (up to 24) random words that you have to string together in order.

You need the mnemonic phrase to restore your wallets in the event you lose your PC or phone. Just download the software to a new device and your wallet will be restored; everything will be fine. This is the same as restoring a backup of your iPhone or Android. You need the password and login details to regain access and restore your apps and content. The mnemonic phrase serves the same purpose to restore your coins.

By the way, sometimes we call the mnemonic phrase a seed phrase, probably because it's a whole lot easier to type and remember.

―――――――――――――――――― WHAT IS A SEED? ――――――――――――――――――

A seed is a list of words, which store all the information needed to recover a crypto wallet. Wallet software will typically generate a seed phrase and instruct the user to write it down on paper.

TYPICAL SEED LENGTH IS 12-24 WORDS

XYZ WALLET

YOUR WALLET GENERATION SEED IS:

check, cake, drive, train, stable, paved, tree, blanket, book, crisp, legal, rock

Please save these 12 words on paper (order is important). This seed will allow you to recover your wallet in case of computer/app failure.

WARNING:

• Never disclose your seed
• Never type it on a website
• Do not store it electronically

SEED PHRASE   BACKUP SEED PHRASE   SEED RECOVERY PHRASE

Now, there's one more thing you need to know—and it's important. Each mnemonic phrase is tied to a specific hardware or software wallet, so you can regain access to it. Only the private key is universal to access your coins. Why? Because your coins are all stored on a public ledger and the private key is your "key" to access those coins on the ledger. As long as you have private keys, you can restore your wallet address to any wallet you like. With only the mnemonic phrase, you can only restore your coins to the specific wallet application you're using.

STORING YOUR PRIVATE KEYS AND MNEMONIC (SEED) PHRASE

 Remember: don't lose your private keys—and don't store your private keys in the cloud

You may have backed up your tax returns—complete with identifying information and banking details—on Google Drive, but it's way too easy for a hacker to pick up your private keys if they're stored anywhere in public. Always use physical copies and don't store those physical copies any place that's easily accessible to others. One of the best places to store it, somewhat ironically, is in a safety deposit box in a bank. At the very least, use a fireproof safe. It may sound crazy but think about how you would feel if you couldn't access your own money. In that light, a fireproof safe doesn't sound so unreasonable now, does it?

The space shuttle has multiple redundant systems for key systems like life support. Obviously, NASA does this for a good reason. Don't

forget backups—plural. You may have heard the saying, "one is none, and two is one"—that applies to backups. If you have one backup, you can still restore your content with confidence. However, with two copies, you have a backup in the event something goes wrong.

So, make a point of having multiple backups of your private keys and seed phrases and keep them in different locations if you can. Try having a paper wallet (in a fireproof safe), a hardware wallet, and one or two software wallets, especially if you have two devices you can use. It might sound excessive, but better safe than sorry.

At the risk of sounding like a nagging parent, if you have one copy in a private safe, put another in a different building, a safety deposit box, or with someone you trust—or all three. You don't have to go crazy with it but having the key in multiple locations will keep you safer in case something goes wrong.

REPLACING A LOST OR STOLEN WALLET

#AskingForAFriend

What if someone I know accidentally loses their hardware wallet?

Lost, damaged, or stolen hardware wallet? Hey, it happens; maybe it's even happened to one of us, but we're not telling. All we can say is that you get the same sinking feeling in the pit of your stomach as when you lose your regular wallet—it feels as though your whole life is gone.

There are two pieces of good news:

1. If you lose access to your hardware wallet, it's possible to restore it, as long as you've backed up your private key or mnemonic phrase.
2. As long as no one else knows your private key or your mnemonic phrase, you're safe. No one will be able to access and steal your coins. It will be useless to everyone else.

The bad news (there's always bad news, isn't there)?

If you don't have the private key or mnemonic phrase, you'll lose your coins. That's painful. It's sitting out there on the public ledger, but you can't access it. It's like losing a winning lottery ticket! We really don't want that to happen to you . . . ever.

Oh, and if you're wondering if it's worth it to buy a whole new hardware wallet if the old one is lost or destroyed, ask yourself this question: can you afford to lose access to your valuable coins? Probably not. Then remember the backup rule: one is none, two is one. Always have a backup of the backup to be safe. And to discover a ton of additional content and details about this, check out our website: www.beleftbehind.com/bonus-content/.

HOW TO KEEP YOUR COINS AND IDENTITY SAFE ON YOUR SMARTPHONE AND PC

Now that you know how to secure your coins with your private keys and mnemonic phrases, there are a few other things you need to do to keep your coins and identity safe when you're accessing your coins online.

DOWNLOAD AND USE A VPN

Remember our goal here is to make sure you're safe. So, the first thing to do is make sure no one can gain unintended access to your PC or smartphone. The best way to do that is to use a Virtual Private Network (VPN).

A VPN creates an encrypted connection between you and whatever websites or apps you're connecting to. This is important because you don't want your data being exposed to anyone. This is a best practice; you should be doing it all the time to make sure your personal data is always as secure as possible.

One of the interesting benefits of using a VPN is that you can connect to a variety of other locations. Your PC or smartphone will appear to be in another country, making it significantly harder to trace back to your PC and your actual location. And who doesn't want to be a ninja?

Now, imagine you're sitting in an Internet café, an airport, or some other public location, and go to connect to a local Internet connection. How do you know the Internet is both valid and safe; how do you know there are no nefarious actors lurking in the ethernet trying to grab your personal details or to hack into your PC? The answer is you don't know. But by installing VPN software, you're immediately creating a mask to make yourself invisible to those up to no good. You're protecting all of your transactions and data at the same time.

Are you concerned enough to act on this? We certainly hope so. Our aim is to make sure you're safe and keep your personal data, your banking details, and your cryptocurrency out of reach from hackers.

To get started all you need to do is sign up to one of the reputable VPN software companies, such as Private Internet Access (PIA) or NordVPN. There are other ones around, and you can search on Google for various VPN comparison reports.

One final point, a VPN will provide added protection if you're out, but you really should do personal, confidential, or monetary transactions from your home or a known safe environment.

CREATE SECURE PASSWORDS

Because so much of what you do in the world of cryptocurrency and in everyday life is connected to your email address, it's really important you have a super secure password.

In fact, when you sign up to any accounts online, you need to create a strong password, and we're not just talking about one simple word that anybody can easily figure out. We're talking about a combination of letters (uppercase and lowercase), numbers, and characters.

Here's a trick:

Come up with a sentence nobody except you knows. Then, take the first letter of each word in that sentence and turn those letters and numbers into a phrase. Get clever to utilize numbers and symbols. Here are a few simple, everyday phrases you can easily work into your sentence that will allow you to incorporate symbols and numbers:

- High 5
- 2 the Store
- @ Lunch
- 4 Us
- You & Me

You can probably think of a lot more. Aim for 12 words (which translates to 12 characters) at a minimum.

Here's an example:

"Yuri went to Mexico in June for vacation and lost his wallet at the restaurant."

Now, let's break that down by using numbers and symbols:

"Yuri went 2 Mexico in June 4 vacation & lost his wallet @ the restaurant."

This translates into the password phrase: Yw2MiJ4v&lhw@tr

That's crazy, right? How many people do you think could crack that password? We're guessing nobody because you won't find many stronger passwords than that. You'd probably be hard pressed to find anybody who could remember that password without knowing the sentence.

Honestly, the first time you try this it might be a little challenging to remember the sentence. It was for us too, but you'll get used to it. Pretty soon, it will be so easy to come up with these types of sentences on your own. What will really surprise you is that you'll remember some of these phrases for the rest of your life.

Also, make sure you create different passwords for all of your accounts and email, so you know all of your accounts are secure.

DON'T USE YOUR MOBILE PHONE NUMBER FOR AUTHENTICATION

With security becoming big business, we often get asked about password manager services that store encrypted passwords offline.

In theory, they sound good, but you can always lose your phone. And don't forget that phones can always be cloned and hacked. If your phone is cloned, the person who cloned it can receive text authorization security codes at the same time you do. That makes it easier for them to reset your passwords and get into your other accounts (or your email).

In other words, if you provide your mobile phone number for authentication, and then your phone gets lost or cloned, hackers can potentially get into your phone; they can see your two-factor authentication (see below); they can access your email and change your passwords; they can see your notes where you stored your private keys on your devices (which you shouldn't have done); they can access your cloud storage drives (where you shouldn't have stored your private keys); and they can access your wallets and clean you out. That's just a list of small things with which to concern yourself. Hopefully it gives you an idea of why using your mobile phone number for authentication can lead to a variety of other problems.

That's why the rule among experts and security advisors is:

  Don't use your mobile phone number for authentication.

USE TWO-FACTOR AUTHENTICATION SOFTWARE

To keep your accounts secure, many systems require a multi-step process to authenticate your identity to login. The login normally requires a standard login of username and password followed by a second step to verify your identity. In some cases, there's even a third authentication step as additional security. Each security step verifies you in a different way. Examples of authentication include email/password, email verification, and using two-factor authentication (2FA) software (sometimes called one-time password, or OTP).

Examples of two-factor authentication software:

- Google Authenticator

- Authy

You can use either application. They're completely interchangeable. The difference is that Google Authenticator only works on one smartphone device and Authy allows you to access your codes across multiple smartphone devices at the same time (useful if you want a family member to have a backup or access).

If you only have Google Authenticator, and you lose your phone, you would have to set everything up all over again, and that's time-consuming. Also, recovering it can be really tough unless you backed up your authenticator settings, too. That's why backups are so critical.

We personally recommend Authy. While not all of you have the luxury of having an extra backup phone lying around at home, one trick is to use a family member's phone as an Authy backup. If something goes wrong, and you need to verify your identity to get into an account, you can call the family member and get the codes. If you have access to a backup copy, you'll feel a lot safer than if you lose the only device that had your authorization codes working. If you've ever had a problem with your PC and lost files, you know what we're talking about. The big difference with cryptocurrency is that we're talking about protecting and being able to access your coins.

 Again, make sure you back up your authentication codes.

For every system you connect with using two-factor authentication, make sure you write down the backup code on a piece of paper because if anything happens, as we discussed above, you'll need those codes to get Google Authenticator and Authy up and running again. If you can't run your authenticator, then you'll have a hard time gaining access again.

You'll also want to make sure you are only able to withdraw your coins from online accounts by using your two-factor authentication. When you go to withdraw your coins, you'll be asked for your two-factor authentication code from Google Authenticator Authy.

Hopefully now you have a pretty good understanding of all the things you need to do to be secure. This is not just for cryptocurrency. This really applies to your entire life when it comes to using the Internet and securing your personal information. Securing your accounts and your devices is the first step. Making sure you have all your private keys and authentication set up is vital to being safe. Next, we'll talk about how to avoid scammers, so you keep your coins safe from those nefarious types.

CHAPTER SEVEN

HOW DO YOU AVOID SCAMMERS?

As discussed earlier, coins are created by groups of people building something they believe adds value to others—they may be part of a registered company, a foundation, or a group of volunteers contributing to a project (open source). Or, they can just be a scammer pretending to be legit in an attempt to steal your money.

For traditional investments (stocks, bonds, real estate), evaluating projects involves looking at the financial health, the viability of the company, and financial statements. If the numbers look good you might be confident the company or project will be a sound investment.

It's not the same for cryptocurrency projects and companies. At least not yet.

Many projects don't have financial statements. The governance around them is entirely different. You might say that, to come up with a more dynamic way of working together, people threw out the rulebook. In doing so, they created a whole new set of challenges for investors, bankers, regulators, and lawyers to work out how to service projects in this new disruptive landscape.

To identify whether a project is real or not, it's important you do some due diligence first—and it can be frustrating and confusing when you're first starting out. Trust us, we know.

DOING YOUR DUE DILIGENCE ON A PROJECT

Before investing in a coin, do as much research about the project as possible. Remember, these projects are not regulated or monitored by financial or government authorities, so you must be more diligent in your research before you invest.

LOOK UP THE TEAM MEMBERS

Are the team members listed on the website? You'll want to know if the team can execute the project. This requires more work than normal, but if you do it well, it will pay off. A good start is to watch YouTube videos about the project. Look for interviews with the founders and what other influencers are saying about the project.

Check out LinkedIn profiles. Do they have a track record or the right level of experience? Look for connections; there's a pretty good chance you know some of the same people; if not, you might know someone who does.

Grab their profile photo and use Google image search to verify they're real. That's cool, right? When we realized we could do that, we found it really helpful!

If you can't find out who's on the team, or you can't verify their photos as being who they say they are, it's probably a scam. Of course, there are exceptions to this; anonymous projects, for example—like our friend Satoshi Nakamoto who launched Bitcoin.

You can also try to reach out to the team, or even contact team members directly through LinkedIn. Call them, email them, or contact them on Telegram or Discord. You'll generally find that people are pretty responsive because they understand the value of developing with other influencers and with their community. If you can't reach the team, if they refuse to show their faces on a video, or even get on a call, then you can be pretty sure it's a scam.

——————— DUE DILIGENCE BEFORE INVESTING ———————

Answering questions like these can help you make the right decision:

Does the project make sense, e.g. does the white paper look good?

Are their social media & communities active?

Do they post their privacy policy and terms & conditions?

Are you connected to anyone who knows them on LinkedIn, to verify them?

Are the company registration and address legit?

What can you find online about the project from media outlets, news sites, medium, etc?

WHAT IS YOUR GUT FEELING?

LOOK AT THE WEBSITE

Does the website have terms and conditions and a privacy policy? We know this sounds obvious, but you would be surprised at how many are copied and pasted from something else or simply not done at all.

Does their website list information about the actual formed company? If they say they have a registered company, confirm their company is really formed and verify the shareholders online. For projects that are just open source we realize you can't check this. But always check everything you can. By all means, look to see what other bloggers and social influencers say about the project.

Does their website list contact information, including an address? If they do, confirm it's legitimate (with the correct post/zip code), use Google maps to look at the address and use the Street View to check the actual location. You wouldn't believe how many projects use fake addresses or use a post/zip code that may be close, but not an exact match. That's their way of trying to look legitimate when they're trying to scam people. They put up something "good enough" so many people will just assume it's nothing to worry about.

Don't just accept their address. Verify it another way to be sure they are not a scam. If it looks wrong, then you should probably re-consider getting involved.

We once tried to verify a company by their UK postcode and address, and it was shocking. Street View in Google Maps gave us an image of an electrical box, but the actual post/zip code was actually nowhere near that location. It was at the local hospital, a 20-minute walk away!

DO THEY HAVE A WORKING PROTOTYPE?

One of the most obvious ways to determine if the project is legitimate is to see if they have anything working, such as a prototype of their app. We often call this prototype a Minimum Viable Product or MVP. At the very least, you should be able to either see something working or be able to download and try it out. It's not the final product; it just gives you a pretty good idea of what the team is building. If you don't like or understand the product, you probably won't invest in it.

> ### LONG ISLAND BLOCKCHAIN COMPANY 🍸
> The Long Island Iced Tea Corp., a beverage company, changed their name to The Long Blockchain Corp. Their stock was down to penny stock level and then suddenly, with the announcement of the name change, it jumped from $1.60 to $7.00 overnight. Sounds good, right? Well, shortly after, they released a statement that basically admitted they had no idea what they were doing. Part of their idea was just to buy a bunch of mining units and mine digital currency. It's not clear what that has to do with their brand. Their shareholders must have thought the same thing because they sold off a bunch of their shares which caused the stock to dip.

We always recommend making sure there's something working so you know what you're buying. If you can't see a working product that they claim exists, it's probably a scam.

LOOK AT THEIR WHITE PAPER

A white paper summarizes what they're doing, why they're doing it, their solution, a technical overview, and a roadmap for the project, along with some legal terms.

One of the first things to look for is the link to their white paper on their website. It might not be there if they have been around for a long time. But for new projects, it's essential. It should always be easily found on the top-level navigation or a link on the homepage. If it's hiding, then sound the alarm! The more information they share the better, because it allows you to validate the project, vision, strategy, structure, and location—all are important. The white paper should focus on the important matters (the product being a major part), the business aspects of the solution, and the technical details.

If you don't understand something about the technology, it's OK to ask around. Blockchain is technical and tricky, but there are a lot of us already involved and we're always happy to help. In fact, if you find a project and want some input, feel free to send us an email at authors@beleftbehind.com. Who knows, perhaps we'll even review the project on our show for you.

Remember, if you read the white paper and it just doesn't make any sense or sounds far-fetched, dreamy, or too good to be true, then it's probably a scam. If it's promising guaranteed returns, run away and don't look back.

OBVIOUS SCAMS TO WATCH OUT FOR

FINANCIAL SCAMS

When you're looking to invest in a project, run away if they're promising any form of dividends, payouts, or guaranteed returns. Dividends are illegal for cryptocurrency projects because they're oftentimes not even businesses and are not regulated to give them out.

One of the most obvious types of scams is called a high-yield investment program (HYIP) or a "hype" or "hip." They promise huge, immediate, and guaranteed returns. These schemes look valid on the surface. They'll claim they will guarantee to give your money back, plus 3% a day, if you invest. The reality is that no one can guarantee returns. Certainly not 3% a day or 10% a week! And when you dig a little deeper, you'll see they're encouraging you to sign up your friends, and your friends' friends, in a pyramid style reward program.

The multi-tier payouts are forms of what is called multi-level marketing. But when you combine it with guaranteed free money, and you don't even know how the money is being made, you should be concerned. When all you know is that you'll make a lot more for getting your friends to sign up their friends, something isn't right. Run away. They're scams. If in doubt, it's best to avoid them or seek out advice from others before jumping in. If it sounds too good to be true, that's because it is.

PHISHING SCAMS

Cybercriminals are always looking for new and innovative ways to deceive you. Phishing scams are one of the most common scams to watch out for. The FBI reports that people lose $30 million a year to phishing scams.

A scammer will contact you via email or a text message by pretending to impersonate another company or product that you already know and trust. They try to trick you to either visit a fake version of a legitimate website or ask you directly to give out your personal information so they can steal your password, bank account number, and other personal details such as identity information or even private keys.

Scammers are always updating their tactics, but you can spot them by looking out for a few key things. They will appear to come from a company you know and trust, such as your bank, online store, credit card company, or social network site. In the body of the email, they'll tell you a story to try to get you to click on a link or open an attachment.

Here are the most common ways they ask you to respond to them to gain access to your information:

- They say they've noticed some suspicious activity or login attempts.
- They claim there's a problem with your account or your payment information.
- They say you must confirm some personal information.
- They send you a fake invoice.
- They ask you to click on a link to make a payment.

- They tell you you're eligible to register for some sort of refund or cash back.

- They offer you a coupon for free stuff.

Here are some key things to look for to help you spot a phishing scam:

- You don't have an account with the company.

- Your name is misspelled or missing, and the email uses bad grammar.

- The email asks for personal information like your Social Security number, national ID, birthday, or password.

- Their email address is an odd variation of the real email address.

- Something about the email just doesn't look right.

Please keep in mind that many of the fake emails look very real. If something doesn't feel right to you, don't click on anything. Contact the company's support desk and open a new browser and physically type in their web address. It's always better to be safe.

FAKE WEBSITES DESIGNED TO STEAL YOUR COINS

Your private keys may keep your wallets secure, but you still need to keep an eye out for fake websites built by hackers, which you might visit by accident.

We've seen several examples of pop-up websites using a fake URL that looked nearly identical to a real website. On these sites, they'll ask you to deposit some Bitcoin in exchange for something in return, like free coins or more Bitcoin, for example. Yes, it may sound ridiculous, expecting to get something for nothing, but we've seen people fall for it. They might be offering you excellent returns for a short-term investment, too. Unfortunately, these scams ask you to input a wallet address and your private key for that wallet. Do you have any alarm bells going off in your head yet? You should!

Many people, who didn't realize these types of websites are not legitimate, have given their private keys and allowed thieves access to their accounts. We don't ever want this to happen to you.

 Never give out your private keys!

Here's our recommendation and takeaway: people will make fake websites of existing websites and try to convince you to invest or deposit your money with them. Sometimes they're exact copies of legitimate websites, but with a fake URL. You're probably thinking that you'd never fall for such a stunt. Good for you. The thing is most people do. Very few of us notice the discrepancies that might tip us off to a fake site.

Here's how you can make yourself less vulnerable:

Look for the padlock. When you enter the URL in a browser's search bar, you should see a little lock—that indicates a secure website.

Check the certificate. If you click on that lock, you can examine the certificate information to verify the site's validity. Certificates are only issued to the legitimate companies (unless the issuer gets hacked, but that's a rarity). If you see an alert saying the certificate does not match the company, that's a bad sign. It may mean you've got an imposter on your hands.

Type in the URL. Always enter the address by hand. Don't click any links sent to you, because it's easy to click on "MyEtherWa11et" without noticing the numbers substituted for letters, which are obvious indications it's a fake website.

Now that you know how to keep your coins safe and what to look for to avoid being scammed, you're probably ready to learn more about buying Bitcoin.

CHAPTER EIGHT

SHOULD I INVEST IN BITCOIN, OR IS IT TOO LATE?

B efore you make that big jump into buying Bitcoin, you probably still have some very practical questions you want answered. Naturally, the biggest question you may have is, "Should I buy Bitcoin or is it too late?"

To be honest, most people starting out in Bitcoin aren't interested (yet) in finding ways to spend it on a coffee or anything else for that matter; they're looking at Bitcoin as a possible investment. That's why we're going to cover the Bitcoin market before we teach you how to buy coins.

In late 2017 and 2018, Bitcoin was on a rollercoaster ride (along with Ethereum, Litecoin, and many other coins). Every time their values went up a little higher, people called it a bubble. Then, just as it went up, it went down. For those new to crypto, those were unsettling times.

Even if you're just discovering Bitcoin now, hearing about a bubble and volatility might make you cautious. You might think you've missed the run as well.

But do you remember when everyone kept saying, "How much can Amazon and Facebook possibly rise; how much can they grow; how much can the share price really go up; how are they going to monetize; how will they get new users and customers?"

Amazon and Facebook built their businesses using the Internet. And, remember, when they both started out a lot of people thought the Internet would go nowhere. People also thought Amazon was overvalued, running at a loss for years. But Amazon leveraged the Internet and has grown to become one of the few companies in the world to be valued at over $1 trillion. Equally, people thought Facebook would never develop into a thriving business and questioned how they would grow and monetize. Yet today, Facebook has three billion users and has announced their intention to launch their own blockchain and cryptocurrency ecosystem called Libra. Those naysayers are probably wishing they had listened to the early investors.

———————————————— STEVE'S STORY ————————————————

When I was getting my master's degree in business, the Internet was just getting started. As part of our master's thesis, we were put into groups and assigned to put together a business plan and pitch our ideas to some venture capitalists (VCs), with the possibility of raising some money. Our plan was to build a search engine for the Internet. Google didn't exist yet and we had some big ideas around how to enable businesses and people to connect. Long story short, the VCs loved our pitch and we won for best business plan. However, they said our plan had no chance of actual success. I remember these exact words: "Listen guys, your plan is great, but this Internet thing is a fad. We've seen things like this come and go, and this Internet thing is no exception." How wrong were they? It's a shame that I listened to them.

Another factor to consider is scarcity (you may recall we mentioned this earlier).

With an absolute limit in the total amount of Bitcoin (21 million coins, in case you forgot), there isn't even enough for everyone on the planet to have one. More importantly, when you compare Bitcoin to gold (another great store of value), gold has a rather unlimited supply. Not only do we still have pockets of unmined gold on the planet, there's a lot more of it sitting in asteroids and other planetary bodies. It might sound silly, but we'll eventually start mining in space, and we'll keep discovering more gold here on Earth. The limited supply of Bitcoin might be interesting for those who see this as a potential growth over gold.

But you don't have to take our word for it.

WHAT INDUSTRY LEADERS ARE SAYING ABOUT BITCOIN

Industry leaders agree that Bitcoin has long-term growth potential.

One of the best ways to decide whether to invest in Bitcoin is to look at what Wall Street analysts are saying. One of our favorites, Thomas J. Lee, CEO at Fundstrat (a research analyst firm in New York) has done a lot of research on Bitcoin, its adoption, and how it's projected to increase in value over time. There are some fantastic videos of him being interviewed on news channels; he's often seen at various conferences and events as well.

Another industry veteran, Mike Novogratz, founder of Galaxy Digital, is another big proponent of Bitcoin and the future of cryptocurrency. He came from the traditional investment firm Fortress before leaving to form his own firm focused on cryptocurrency investments. He's regularly covered in the press and you can read all about his views and where he thinks Bitcoin is going (you'll be happy to see where he thinks it's going, too).

Another industry leader and Silicon Valley investor to check out is Tim Draper. He's an avid investor who has invested in companies such as Skype, Tesla, and Twitter as well as blockchain and cryptocurrency startups such as Coinbase. He's made a number of very big predictions including that Bitcoin will rise to $250,000 by 2023. That's a pretty big target, but it comes from someone who has a lot of knowledge and experience in the investment world and in Bitcoin.

INDICATORS THAT CRYPTOCURRENCY IS GOING MAINSTREAM

Of course, you may simply be waiting for cryptocurrency to go mainstream.

Sure, from a user growth perspective, Bitcoin is just beginning; many of the tech and social media companies are much more mature. Out of over seven billion people, maybe 50 million have cryptocurrency. That's about 0.7% of the world's population.

But if you look closely, you'll see it might not be long before blockchain and cryptocurrency are mainstream.

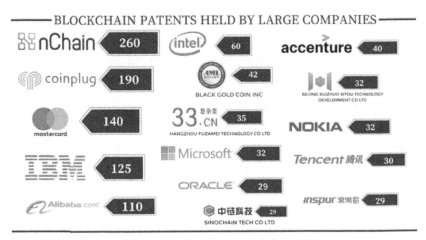

Source: https://www.cintelliq.com/research/report/blockchain/

Here are a few indicators of how cryptocurrency and Bitcoin are going mainstream:

1. News Coverage: We see Bitcoin and cryptocurrency coverage in the news every day, even on major outlets such as *Forbes* and CNBC. Many major companies have patents in blockchain, which continues to create more coverage in the press. Cryptocurrency has even been a subject in several movies, TV shows, and some documentaries. Any fans of television shows like *The Big Bang Theory, Silicon Valley,* and *The OA* (on Netflix) might have noticed that Bitcoin and Ethereum have been a topic of discussion.

2. Massive investments: Did you know that significantly more money was invested in cryptocurrency projects in 2018 than traditional startups in technology? Blockchain and cryptocurrency are clearly having an enormous impact on where venture capital money is being invested.

3. Acceptance as payment: People get paid in Bitcoin all the time. (Although, some people unfortunately turned it down in the earlier days.)

WHO KNEW? NOT LILY ALLEN...

Right at the start of the Bitcoin craze, singer Lily Allen admitted that someone had offered to pay her hundreds of thousands of Bitcoin to stream a gig on Second Life.

LILY ALLEN @lilyallen

About 5 years ago someone asked me to stream a gig live on second life for hundreds of thousNds of bitcoins, "as if" I said. #idiot #idiot

♡ 798 11:22 PM - Jan 5, 2014

○ 618 people are talking about this

Lily Allen, if you're reading this, we feel your pain. (You would have been a billionaire!)

4. Acceptance by nations: Cryptocurrency, not just Bitcoin, is broadly recognized as valid legal currency in countries such as Belarus, Estonia, Ukraine, and Sweden. Japan uses it widely as a standard currency. And people within

Venezuela have been adopting DASH coin, amongst others, in light of their economic meltdown.

5. Adoption by major companies: Like we said, if Facebook is rolling out their own cryptocurrency and launching Libra, watch how quickly the rest of the world adapts and adopts. Overstock has already started accepting it. Expedia travel allows you to pay for flights with Bitcoin. Microsoft Xbox allows you to pay with Bitcoin, too. So, you see, more is happening than you probably realized.

Now, as most investors and early adopters know, growth comes from knowing when to hold them, and when to sell.

KNOW WHEN TO HODL

No, that's not a typo. HODL is cryptocurrency slang for holding onto your coins instead of selling them. The term goes back to a discussion on Bitcoin Chat in 2013 where a forum user posted "I am hodling" misspelling the word, holding. This led to a lengthy discussion about the typo. In the end, the term stuck, and everyone has kept the word HODL, when talking about holding onto your Bitcoin and cryptocurrency. Someone even came up with an acronym for it (Hold On for Dear Life).

Some analysts say Bitcoin is worth holding onto for a long time. We agree, simply because the current number of users is relatively small compared to total size of the world population. There will be more and more interest that will only gain momentum as more people become aware of what's going on and invest in it. As more apps are available that make it easier for people to get started, you're going to see more people jumping in, too.

OUR RESPONSE TO THE NAYSAYERS

Is Bitcoin a bubble?

One of the big naysayers of Bitcoin is Jamie Dimon, CEO of JPMorgan. He compared Bitcoin to the Tulip Mania bubble. If you look up "tulip mania" you'll find out how the price of tulips climbed incredibly high before collapsing in 1637. It's kind of a bizarre analogy, but it's what he said. He also said:

"Right now, these crypto things are kind of a novelty. People think they're kind of neat. But the bigger they get, the more governments are going to close them down . . . It's creating something out of nothing that to me is worth nothing." – Jamie Dimon, CEO, JPMorgan, September 2017, *Fortune*

Ironically, JPMorgan has since turned around and launched their own coin, the JPM Coin. We're guessing he doesn't think it's a bubble anymore.

James Bullard, President of the St. Louis Federal Reserve (part of the National Federal Reserve in the US) said:

"I want to view cryptocurrencies of various types as new entrants into the ongoing global currency competition." - James Bullard, the President of the St. Louis Federal Reserve, July 2019

So, if there really was a bubble, then it wouldn't really make sense for the US Federal Reserve to be concerned about the future of the US dollar, would it?

Here are a few other thoughts for cryptocurrency cynics . . .

FOR THE NAYSAYERS WHO THINK BITCOIN WILL COME TO ITS DEMISE

The only way we could imagine Bitcoin going to zero would be if everyone stopped using it or governments shut down every mining operation in existence. These arguments seem rather unlikely given the amount of adoption taking place. A major coordinated effort would be required to shut down all mining operations around the world. As long as people continue buying and using it, adoption will continue.

#AskingForAFriend

Is Bitcoin a Ponzi scheme?

No. Accusing Bitcoin of being a Ponzi scheme is one of the most common arguments against cryptocurrency, mostly because it's misunderstood.

In case you're not familiar, the Ponzi scheme was invented in 1920 by Charles Ponzi (and made truly famous by Bernie Madoff in 2013). The scheme is designed to lure investors in with guaranteed high returns with little to no downside. In reality, the returns are generated by newer investors whose investments are used to pay out to earlier investors. This works until either an early investor redeems their funds (asks for their initial investments to be returned) or when there are not enough new investors to continue paying out the earlier ones, causing the scheme to collapse.

By contrast, Bitcoin is fully decentralized and there are no promises of returns. There isn't anyone to invest in and there are no payouts of any form. Bitcoin is accessible from many places including trading exchanges and from ATMs and not from a single person or entity with whom you're investing.

Despite these facts, there are still people who make the argument that Bitcoin is a Ponzi scheme or a pyramid. They try to single out Satoshi Nakamoto as the person or group at the top and those who got in early are the ones making money off the latest groups to jump in.

It's hard for us to begin to understand how the comparison is even being made or justified. Bitcoin is trading on over 250 trading exchanges around the world in a free market economy. It's been legalized in a variety of countries around the world as a form of legal tender, and is now seen as a threat to the US as part of the global currency competition.

Perhaps when you hear someone refer to Bitcoin as a Ponzi, just hand them a copy of this book and help us educate them.

FOR THE NAYSAYERS WHO THINK BITCOIN LEADS TO MONEY LAUNDERING

What's interesting is how much the media and banking executives love to claim cryptocurrency is only used for nefarious activities. Perhaps they're using scaremongering to keep us out, so they can get in?

Well, here's an interesting fact to serve as a response: there is far more money being laundered in fiat than in crypto, by a very large proportion.

FIAT
ESTIMATED
$800 M - $2T A YEAR VIA
BANK TRANSFERS
(ACCORDING TO
BLOOMBERG)

CRYPTO
ESTIMATED $91 M OVER 2 YEARS
VIA CRYPTOCURRENCY
EXCHANGE SHAPESHIFT
(ACCORDING TO WALL STREET JOURNAL)

$800 M - $2T

$91 M

Source: https://www.newsbtc.com/2019/02/04/banks-are-better-than-bitcoin-when-it-comes-to-money-laundering/

Let's face it, cryptocurrency is a threat to the status quo for banks because it eliminates the middleman and puts you in control of your money. Is that same as money laundering? No, but if the banks can find a clever way to create some fear and maintain control, then it stands to reason they will do so, until they adopt.

FOR THE NAYSAYERS WHO THINK BITCOIN IS TOO VOLATILE AN INVESTMENT

Sure, the value of Bitcoin will rise and fall. So will Amazon shares. In fact, take a look at the amount of volatility investors experienced in the early days of Amazon.

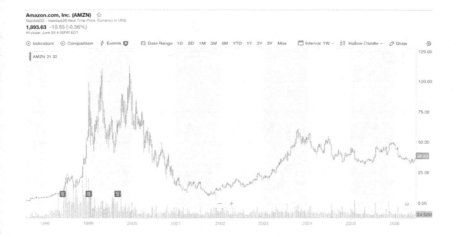

Yet, those who have held on to Amazon, despite the rise and falls, have made a lot of money.

If you look at the charts of Bitcoin from its early days, you can see a similar comparison in the price movement.

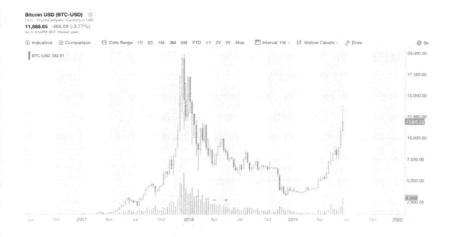

As companies grow and become more mainstream, their stock prices tend to stabilize. We believe Bitcoin will do the same as main- stream adoption takes place over time.

CHAPTER NINE

HOW DO YOU ACTUALLY BUY BITCOIN?

A t this point, you have a good understanding of blockchain and cryptocurrency. You understand the volatility and how it's played out in other disruptive companies/opportunities. Now that you've made it this far, you're probably itching to get involved and you want to know how to get started.

So, let's get started.

The first step is exchanging your local currency (USD, euros, GBP, yen, or whatever currency you're starting with) to Bitcoin. You do this by going to an exchange. The process of opening an account on an exchange is a lot like opening a new bank account. You have to verify your identity; then, once your account is approved, you can deposit your money.

We're going to break it down, step-by-step.

STEP 1: REGISTER AND SECURE YOUR ACCOUNT ON AN EXCHANGE

When you're just starting out, and you only have fiat (like USD), you need to register an account with an exchange so you can buy Bitcoin.

You have numerous options, all around the world; some examples include Coinbase, Gemini, Bittrex International, and Binance Jersey.

To register, you'll provide your name and email address (you may be asked for other information as well, such as your birthday and home address); you'll also create a password (make sure you create something unique and really secure, because this is where you'll be storing your coins—remember our trick).

On that note, when you put your coins on an exchange, they will not provide you with a private key to keep your coins safe. You must trust the exchange to keep your coins safe for you (similar to how you trust a bank to do it for you). It's not ideal and we know how much we've stressed the importance of managing your coins yourself. Our advice is never put more on an exchange than you're planning on trading. You can always move them offline to a hardware wallet once you have made your investments and are ready to hold them.

Next, you'll be able to set up additional security features such as two-factor authentication. We highly recommend you do this right away, so you get your account locked down, safe and secure. And remember: don't use your mobile phone for verification. We can't emphasize enough the importance of these steps. The more secure your account, the safer you will be.

STEP 2: VERIFY YOUR IDENTITY WITH KYC (KNOW YOUR CUSTOMER)

Now that your account is setup and secure, you'll need to verify your identity. This is the same process you follow when you open a bank account or other service where you'll be sending and receiving money.

When you sign up with an exchange, the verification process is called KYC (Know Your Customer). You'll be asked to provide a copy of your passport or other form of national identity. You may also be asked to do a biometric scan where you use their app or website to scan your face for additional authentication and verification.

This is being done to secure your account, so hackers won't be able to gain access to your personal accounts. It's also required to protect against money laundering. But don't worry, the data you provide is only being provided to the exchange, who still must comply with all of laws around data security and privacy.

After you supply a copy of your national ID, many of the exchanges ask for additional forms of verification. They may ask you to provide a selfie along with today's date and the account number for the account you just opened. You'll need to take out a piece of paper, write the information down, and hold up your passport or national ID in the picture as well. This is somewhat unique to the cryptocurrency exchanges, but don't be surprised if you start seeing this being added to other systems you use.

Once you have submitted your identity information, you'll receive verification in as little as 15 to 20 minutes or, in some cases, within a day. Once you get your email confirmation, you're approved and ready to start buying Bitcoin and trading other coins.

STEP 3: BUYING YOUR FIRST BITCOIN WITH FIAT

You're now ready to start buying some Bitcoin. Depending on the exchange, you'll be able to buy your first Bitcoin with a credit card, a debit card, an instant bank transfer, or a wire transfer of funds to the exchange. Your choices will depend on the local country, the exchange you're using, and local regulations for that exchange.

Depending on your credit card limits and the price of Bitcoin, you may prefer to do a wire transfer instead of trying to buy it with your credit card. If you're buying Bitcoin by sending fiat to the exchange through a wire transfer, then you'll have to wait until the funds arrive, are cleared and confirmed.

If you're buying Bitcoin with a debit or credit card, the process is generally very straightforward. There may be some short delays to confirm the transaction, but the exchanges are really good about keeping you informed via emails and system notifications.

That's it. You're now the proud owner of anywhere from 0.00000001 Bitcoin to something higher.

Congratulations!

SELLING YOUR COINS BACK TO FIAT

Good news: if you linked your bank account or did a wire transfer, you'll be able to sell your Bitcoin back to fiat and then wire that money back to your bank account. It's really simple.

If, however, you bought your Bitcoin with a debit or credit card and the exchange doesn't offer a fiat withdrawal service, you'll need to find another exchange that provides services to enable you to sell Bitcoin and wire your funds back to your bank account. Don't worry too much about this; the cryptocurrency world is evolving quickly, with more and more services coming online.

Now that you have your first Bitcoin, let's look at how you can send it.

CHAPTER TEN

HOW DO YOU SEND YOUR FIRST BITCOIN?

O ne of the most common questions people ask us is also one of their biggest worries: how do I send my cryptocurrency? The reason they're worried is because the process is completely foreign. Those long strings of letters and numbers that make up the wallet addresses are scary for many people—they aren't comfortable or familiar.

With a bank account, you have a debit card tied to your account number. It's an object you know precisely how to use. But with cryptocurrency, your wallet address looks techy, it feels unsafe, and can give you a sinking feeling in your belly that you might be doing something wrong. But rest assured, you aren't doing anything wrong, and we're going to explain exactly how it works so you feel comfortable doing it. Ready? Here we go.

Let's say you've got some coins in your wallet and you want to send them to a friend.

To send coins to your friend, you need to ask for your friend's wallet address. You'll then use your wallet software or hardware to send the coins to the wallet address your friend gave you.

Once you click send, the transaction will be recorded on the ledger in the blockchain. The transaction will be confirmed multiple times, one block at a time, by the miners whose computer equipment will confirm your transaction. Once the confirmation process is complete, it's all done. Your coins have safely been sent to your friend—and they'll display on your friend's wallet address.

SENDING BITCOIN ANY TIME OF THE DAY OR NIGHT

Our friend, Jeremy, recently contacted us because he wanted to send some Bitcoin from one wallet address to another (to his friend), but he was worried he might be doing something wrong and didn't want to make any mistakes. We talked him through the entire process and wanted to share that with you. The conversation went something like this:

> Jeremy: "Hey Steve, I want to send 0.1 BTC (Bitcoin) to a friend of mine. I just want to be sure when I send it, he gets the correct amount and I have a record of the transaction. How can I prove this; what am I not understanding?"

> Steve: "Hey Jeremy, sure; let me describe the process. It's pretty straightforward. You go to the Send function inside your wallet. Copy and paste the wallet address your friend gave you. Make sure you're sending 0.1 BTC. And click 'send.'"

> Jeremy: "I can do that. I have to add his address to my book (whitelisted). What does that mean?"

> Steve: "It means you should add the wallet address to your list of known addresses and label it with your friend's name. That way, in the future you know who that address belongs to and you know you're sending it to the right person."

> Jeremy: "How will I receive confirmation of the transaction?"

Steve: "When you confirm and send the Bitcoin, you'll be given a transaction ID (which is a long string of letters and numbers). It might look a bit scary, but don't worry; it's just a confirmation. You'll use it to lookup your transaction online, to verify. You can send it to your friend so he can track the transaction as well."

Jeremy: "OK, that makes sense. But where do I go to find that transaction and watch it go through. It's something like tracking a parcel, right?"

Steve: "Exactly. You can go to blockchain.com, for example, which is where the Bitcoin explorer is. The explorer (the term we use in crypto) is the place where you can track the transactions. You just need to copy and paste the transaction ID into the Search field, and it will show you the transaction. It will show your wallet address (from), your friend's wallet address (to), and the amount that was sent."

Jeremy: "And how do I know my wallet address? I know, stupid question. I feel silly asking, but I don't fully understand this and it's a bit scary."

Steve: "Actually, it's not stupid at all. To find your wallet address, click on "Receive" on your wallet app; it will show your wallet address. This will be the recipient address your friend will see—where the Bitcoin came from."

Steve: "You can also just copy your wallet address and paste it into the Bitcoin explorer. It will show you all the transactions for your wallet address, both sent and received."

Jeremy: "OK, I'll follow the steps you've laid out. Hopefully I don't mess it up and I'll get back to you in a couple. Thanks!"

Steve: "As long as you send to your friend's BTC wallet address you'll be fine. And if you're worried, just send me a screenshot before you send it and I'll verify it for you. "

Steve: "Also, remember, after you click send, it will take a few minutes before it shows up on the blockchain explorer. That's perfectly normal. You're just waiting for the transaction to be recorded into the blockchain. "

Jeremy: "Great! All completed, I think. Can you look? [screenshot with the transaction ID]"

Steve: "Perfect! Great job mate!"

Jeremy: "Damn, it's not easy when you don't know exactly what you're doing. Ha-ha. But that really helped me. I still have a lot to learn. It's great to have friends like you to help me out. Thank you! I feel so much more confident now. It really is so much easier than I thought. Thanks again!"

As you see, it's not so bad. Yes, it might be a bit intimidating. But as long as you copy and paste the wallet address where you are sending the funds, you'll be just fine. We believe this will eventually be replaced with easier and more comfortable ways to send crypto in the future, such as using an email address inside an app. But for now, just trust us when we say everything is OK; once you get started, you're going to open up a whole new world.

WHY IT'S WORTH GETTING OVER YOUR TECH PHOBIA

You probably know the feeling of having bills to pay at the end of the month and waiting for your paycheck to come. Any delay can lead to a bunch of problems, including a late payment (which causes additional fees) or not enough spending money for the weekend. Add a payment processing error in the mix, and it's all the more stressful.

Then there's the fact that when money comes into your bank account, it's not actually cleared (spendable) until the following business day. That's probably the most frustrating thing about banking—you can see your money, but you can't actually spend it, especially when you need it!

And the problem doesn't stop with accessing your pay in a timely fashion. The banking world is equally frustrating when it comes to sending money to friends or family.

Typically, to send funds, you use a service like Western Union or PayPal; you might wire the money from your bank account locally; or, for international transactions, use an intermediary such as SWIFT (Society for Worldwide Interbank Financial Telecommunication). The funds then go through a process involving multiple intermediaries to settle and clear the funds. This can often take a few days, even longer with weekends and holidays; and each intermediary adds additional costs and a potential point of failure.

In addition, there are always restrictions set by the banks: the amount being sent, destination (country), identification requirements, or regulatory restrictions. That means your friend or family member in urgent need of money, may be stuck waiting a few days (if the funds are received at all).

So, when it comes to accessing your pay or sending money to someone, why should you have to wait more than a few minutes to receive the funds—especially when it's being sent electronically?

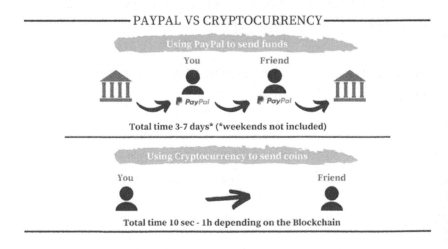

PAYPAL VS CRYPTOCURRENCY

Using PayPal to send funds

You   Friend

Total time 3-7 days* (*weekends not included)

Using Cryptocurrency to send coins

You   Friend

Total time 10 sec - 1h depending on the Blockchain

Sending coins is completely automated. You don't have to wait for the money to be transferred. You don't have to deal with a bank. It shows up in minutes and is immediately available to spend.

Your coins are simply transmitted, sent, and received safely and quickly every time to anyone, anytime, anywhere in the world. And there has never been a report of a send/receive failure since cryptocurrency started.

SAY GOODBYE TO BIG TRANSACTION FEES

It's crazy to think we haven't modernized our banking systems to automate transactions and allow us to send and receive funds instantaneously. They're all electronic transactions, yet the fees we incur for wiring money internationally remain incredibly high and inefficient.

As you may know, PayPal transactions aren't actually free. Neither are the costs for receiving wire transfers to your bank account in most cases. (International transactions are even more expensive.) The bank acts as the intermediary, and they take their cut. It's a small percentage, but those percentages add up, especially when you're talking about more and more money.

With cryptocurrency, not only are the transactions nearly instantaneous, the transaction fees are a fraction of any banking fees.

Here's an example:

To send the equivalent of $5,000 from the US to India, you'll be required to use SWIFT as an intermediary (since your local bank isn't on the same network as the bank in India). This will, of course, come with an additional fee for the intermediary to process your transaction. You'll also have to pay for the wire transfer (handling fee), costs for conversion from US dollars to Indian rupee, and some service fees for convenience. Sending the $5,000 can often amount to $50 or more in transaction fees depending on actual size of the transaction.

Send the equivalent of $5,000 using Bitcoin or another cryptocurrency, and you'll pay anywhere from a few cents (USD) to a few dollars, no matter where you send it. Quite honestly, we wish we would have been as acronym savvy as SWIFT; we would have invented our own: Bank Inter-monetary Transactions Confirmed on International Network (BITCOIN)—only kidding.

Hopefully, you see why using the blockchain to send cryptocurrency is so much more attractive.

CHAPTER ELEVEN

HOW DO YOU PICK YOUR NEXT INVESTMENT IN ALTCOINS?

N ow that you've got your first Bitcoin, you might be considering how to invest in alternative coins. We love how you're beginning to see the possibilities. With several thousand coins listed on exchanges (and counting), here's a look at how to determine what coins to buy.

The easiest place to find a list of coins is on coin market cap websites such as Coinmarketcap.com, CoinPaprika.com, and CoinGecko.com. Similar to websites like Yahoo Finance or Google Finance, these websites are for anyone who wants to find more information about coins.

STEP 1: START WITH WHAT YOU KNOW

Look for companies and projects that do something you can understand.

We got our start buying the most well-known coins—the ones with the biggest communities and support. When you look at the top coins by market cap, you start to get an idea where we're heading. Bitcoin,

Ethereum, Bitcoin Cash, and Litecoin are all popular coins with the largest market cap. They have large communities and continue to gain adoption into the mainstream. What makes choosing these coins so easy: information is readily available. You'll be able to get involved and learn a lot, and that's what you want.

STEP 2: FIND THE HOTTEST PROJECTS BY FOLLOWING THE EXPERTS

Everyone wants to invest in the hottest projects. Of course, much like investing in the stock market, finding the hottest investments can be a challenge. For insight when we were first getting started, we went to a private chat group and asked for advice. They said, "Follow five YouTubers who cover projects, and you'll find the best ones for sure."

FOLLOW THE BIGGEST INFLUENCERS ON YOUTUBE

Honestly, this piece of advice is too good not to pass on to you. We spend a lot of time making sure we provide reviews, interviews, and opinions about projects. Why not benefit from our research (and that of other experts, as well)?

We follow a variety of YouTubers. Some really focus on coins and identifying hot projects; some interview a variety of project founders to help you learn more about what's happening in blockchain and cryptocurrency. We're one of many YouTube channels out there. To get you started, here are a few you might consider following (this list is in no way exhaustive):

- Ian Balina
- Crypto Beadles

- Crypto Crow

- Michael Nye (podcaster and Tweeter)

- Ivan on Tech

- Crypto Face (Market Cipher and how to invest in Bitcoin)

- The Coin Chat (shameless plug)

FOLLOW THE BIGGEST INFLUENCERS ON TWITTER

Ironically, some of the best people to follow are the ones who run the big projects, including:

- Charlie Lee from Litecoin

- Roger Ver from Bitcoin Cash

- Satoshi Nakamoto, founder(s) of Bitcoin

- The Winklevoss Brothers, founders of Gemini Exchange

- John McAfee, investor in a variety of cryptocurrency projects

Check out our website for a list of influencers at www.beleftbehind.com/influencers.

READ VARIOUS ANALYSTS' PUBLICATIONS

Hacker Noon is an outstanding publication that provides a lot of great market analysis and content. Medium articles are another great place to see what people are saying.

Thomas J. Lee (we mentioned him earlier), from Fundstrat, is also a great source of information. His firm provides a range of analytical reports. He is regularly seen on CNBC and on YouTube.

Determining which project to invest in requires a tremendous amount of research. It really helps if you're tapped into the communities. We admit that it's hard to find this information, so you really have to know where to look.

STEP 3: ANALYZE THE PROJECTS

Before you start buying coins on exchanges (the ones recommended by the experts, or not), you've got to take responsibility for analyzing them. There are a few ways to do just that.

One is by looking at their tokenomics, which is probably a term you've never heard before. The other two may be more familiar: technical analysis and fundamental analysis. They involve the sort of research you'd do when looking at traditional companies that are trading on a stock market.

TOKENOMICS

When we talk about tokenomics, we're talking about how the coin is being used within the DApp (that's a decentralized app) or their product or service. We often refer to this as the utility or uses of the coin.

Remember when we compared tokens to loyalty or rewards cards from your favorite shops, or cashback rewards credit cards? Way back when, we were describing the different kinds of coins.

OK, it's time for a little refresher.

Many people ask about the difference between a token and a coin. The answer is reasonably simple. A coin is the term used when talking about currency for making payments. When a project creates a DApp, there will be other ways the coin can be used for utility. In those instances, we refer to the coin as a token. Yes, it's a bit silly to have two different words for describing different ways a coin is used. And, quite

honestly, it confuses a lot of people. We just want you to be aware of it in case it comes up when you're looking to invest.

The point of the token—the entire goal for every cryptocurrency project—is to develop a model where the token has utility value, or real use cases that enable the token to be used within the DApp. Remember, we're not talking about a company that operates by accepting dollars or yen. We're talking about a major shift where companies are literally running their business on their own token. Tokenomics is the very core of how token models are defined and how they demonstrate real business use cases (or don't).

Are you still confused? Don't worry. We're going to give you an example of a tokenomics model that will hopefully clear things up for you.

One of the best examples of a tokenomics model is how Binance, the cryptocurrency exchange, has utilized their token to run their own ecosystem.

Binance, like many other exchanges, provides a centralized place where investors can buy coins for new projects.

Binance's token is called BNB. Here's the first way the BNB tokens are used: every time you trade (buy and sell) on the exchange, there's a fee for each transaction. Binance encourages people to pay for their transaction fees with the BNB, and they offer discounts on the trading fees for doing so. They're using their own coin as a token with a transaction fee as a utility function.

Second: when you trade in cryptocurrency, sometimes there's not an even exchange in value between the coins and you end up with "dust" in your account—small particles of coins you can't trade or use. So, guess what Binance offers to do? They "sweep up the dust" in exchange for some BNB coins! This is the second way they use their token; it results in tons of dust from users, adding up to a lot of coins for Binance.

The third use: Binance enables you to make early investments into new projects through their "Launchpad" service. Similar to mainstream crowdfunding, the Binance platform allows early access to buy coins for blockchain projects (to raise money and invest in them, in other words). And you can use your BNB tokens (coins) to make this investment.

Binance has found and created multiple use cases for their BNB coin to give real utility value to the coin as a token. When you see multiple uses, you're looking at something with real legs.

Now that you've learned a bit about tokenomics, let's look at the more traditional forms of analysis.

TECHNICAL ANALYSIS

In simplest terms, technical analysis is a process and technique used by traders to identify trading opportunities based upon trends and patterns. We won't go into great detail here, namely because this is a very deep topic and you can read all about it on a variety of websites and online courses.

However, we've found that some of the more traditional ways you do technical analysis don't necessarily work when you analyze coins. There are a few explanations for this. First off, there are a number of early investors (referred to as whales). There's often talk that these whales tend to have more power to move the markets. There may be some truth in this, but in reality, this occurs in traditional markets as well.

Another factor: "cryptocurrency never sleeps"—an expression you'll often hear. It refers to the fact that trading is running every hour of every day, all year round, including public holidays. The implication is that you get a lot of different countries, groups, and individuals all trading in a variety of ways, at the same time—something you wouldn't see in traditional financial markets. With a larger number of traders and locations, it's entirely possible this affects the trends and patterns.

One of our YouTuber friends, a trader who started in traditional trading and moved into cryptocurrency trading, has identified a whole range of patterns in how Bitcoin moves and trades, which are unique.

Not only has he identified these patterns, he has built an entire show about them on YouTube called *Crypto Face*. He's even created his own technical indicators called Market Cipher, which provide a level of technical analysis not achieved through other traditional indicators.

FUNDAMENTAL ANALYSIS

You can get a good feel for a possible investment opportunity by watching the news. You see a big merger, for example, and a flag goes up. Pay close attention, the stock prices are about to fluctuate. Walmart suddenly signs a big contract, and you take a closer look. It may be time to invest in the new supplier. In traditional investing, we call this sort of information the fundamentals.

You can track the fundamentals in blockchain projects, too. Here are some things to look for:

- What is the project doing?

- Does it make sense? Have they launched a product?

- Does the product work?

- How many people are using the product?

- How much money are they making from sales of that product?

- Do they have offices or are they a group scattered all over the world?

- Are laws or regulations changing that will affect their business or project plans?

- Are there any major announcements coming out from regulators such as the SEC, FCA, or other regulatory bodies?

- Are governments providing laws or guidance to ease adoption or are they creating barriers to prevent progress from occurring?

Scour newsletters and Medium articles to learn all the basics about the project. Try to evaluate it as much as you can, much like you would for a traditional business (understanding there's still a major paradigm shift in how you evaluate them, too).

- How transparent are they about the project or business they run?

- Does the project have a good following?

- What kind of press does it get?

- Are news agencies interested in the project?

- Have any of the contributors or employees been interviewed on CNBC or *Forbes*?

- Who has invested in the project and who is backing it?

And the list goes on . . .

As an example, here are some really cool fundamentals we found about Theta Token. The project is backed by Sony and Samsung. Sequoia Capital China and the founders of Twitch and YouTube are also involved. This information alone is powerful because it gives some validation that the project has a good foundation and support. There's a lot more Theta Token has going on. And this information was readily available just by looking at their website and LinkedIn and checking their Twitter pages and social media.

The point is, all aspects of a project are important to look into if you really want to make a good decision on what to buy for long term HODLing (remember, HODLing started as a typo in a chat group that turned into the term we use for holding our coins/investments).

In short, the best advice we can give you is to make sure you do your homework. If you're still struggling, you can always contact us at www.beleftbehind.com for help. You'll also find lots of free bonus content on our website that may provide you the answers you're looking for.

Now that you've got an understanding of how to analyze coins, we're going to tell you how to find the coins you may want to invest in, and how to get your Bitcoin onto an exchange where you can buy those coins to start trading.

STEP 4: INVESTING IN A PROJECT

There are two ways you can invest into a project. Either you can invest early before the project's coins are trading on an exchange, or you can invest after the coin is trading.

INVESTING AT THE GROUND LEVEL (CROWDFUNDING)

If you want to get in at the ground level—when a hot project first issues their coin, before they're publicly available for trading—you can participate in the crowdfunding process by buying their coins. For getting in early, you'll receive bonus coins or discounts on the price of the coin. You're buying a coin, which you can spend or use within that project's app or hold as an investment.

Just be aware that when you invest in a blockchain project and purchase coins, the coins are not the same as equity or shares. They do not have any voting rights in a company. Also, you won't receive any form of dividends from profits like you would for investing in a company. In fact, coins are oftentimes not even tied to a company.

The most well-known types of crowdfunding are:

- Initial Coin Offering (ICO): Popular from 2016 to mid-2018, the first way that cryptocurrency projects raised money through crowdfunding

- Initial Exchange Offering (IEO): Popular starting in late 2018 to early 2019, is a managed crowdfunding model, like Indiegogo or

Kickstarter, where the exchanges provide a service for investors to gain early access to invest in projects

- Security Token Offering (STO): Started in mid-2018 to create a highly regulated environment for high net worth investors to do early investments

We've got a lot more detail about these crowdfunding models on our website: www.beleftbehind.com/bonus-content/.

INVESTING AFTER A PROJECT IS TRADING ON AN EXCHANGE

Each project's coins are eventually listed on exchanges. In the next chapter, we'll tell you exactly how to find the coins and start trading them.

CHAPTER TWELVE

HOW DO YOU FIND COINS AND START TRADING THEM?

Here's a question we get every time we start talking about cryptocurrency investments. How do I know which exchange a coin is on?

Actually, finding which coin is traded where is probably a lot easier than it sounds. Every coin is listed on one or several exchanges. Every coin is also listed on websites that summarize information about the coin, including price and market cap. The most popular websites are CoinMarketCap, Coin Paprika, and CoinGecko.

WHICH EXCHANGE IS MY COIN ON?

Check out these websites that provide overviews of many coins:

CoinGecko: coingecko.com
CoinMarketCap: coinmarketcap.com
WorldCoinIndex: www.worldcoinindex.com
Coin Paprika: coinpaprika.com

When you visit these sites and search for a coin, the Markets section for that coin will show you all the exchanges where the coin is trading. If you look up Ripple on CoinMarketCap, for example, the first column shows it's traded on a variety of exchanges, including ZB.com, BitMart, ZBG, and UPbit (among others). The coins that Ripple (XRP) trades against are also listed. These are referred to as trade pairs. You can often trade a coin against more than just Bitcoin but, for the sake of simplicity, we're just following the trade against Bitcoin for now.

——————INFORMATION ABOUT WHERE MY COIN IS LISTED——————

XRP Markets

#	Source	Pair	Volume (24h)	Price	Volume (%)
1	ZB.COM	XRP/BTC	$47,473,545	$0.300684	10.40%
2	BitMart	XRP/USDT	$29,244,531	$0.301428	6.41%
3	ZBG	XRP/USDT	** $27,061,818	$0.300727	5.93%
4	UPbit	XRP/KRW	$16,630,252	$0.294799	3.64%
5	Exrates	XRP/BTC	$14,108,973	$0.304655	3.09%
6	BCEX	XRP/CKUSD	$13,435,119	$0.289447	2.94%
7	HitBTC	XRP/USDT	$13,422,762	$0.301084	2.94%
8	Binance	XRP/USDT	$12,482,856	$0.301518	2.73%

CHOOSING AN EXCHANGE TO BUY A COIN

The process of choosing an exchange can be overwhelming. There are too many, and you've probably never heard of most of them. Our recommendation: gauge the exchanges by the volume of trading taking place. When you look at these market cap websites for coins, they'll show you the coin and all the trading pairs available for that coin.

Continuing the example, above, let's say you want to buy Ripple (XRP). You can see Bitcoin to Ripple (XRP/BTC)—an example trade pair—with the trade volume. You can also see Ripple trade pairs to USD Tether (USDT), and even Korean won (KRW). Our suggestion is to pick the top two exchanges that have the most trading by volume and start there—which, for our example, would be ZB.com and BitMart.

There's no point going to the smaller exchanges because there isn't as much volume and that often makes trading a lot harder (fewer buyers and sellers). These types of exchanges are similar to eTrade, Ameritrade, or any other online trading platforms you might use to trade stocks, bonds, or other assets.

GETTING YOUR BITCOIN ONTO THE EXCHANGE TO START TRADING

Let's say you want to buy Ripple with Bitcoin, making our trade pair XRP/BTC.

The exchange where you bought your Bitcoin won't have every single coin that is traded. Assuming it doesn't have Ripple, your next step will be to send your Bitcoin to one or more exchanges where you can buy Ripple (or another hot coin you've spotted). Just send your Bitcoin from your wallet to your wallet address on the exchange where you want to trade just like we spoke about earlier.

You'll go through the same process of signing up for each exchange like you did when you bought your first Bitcoin. Once you have signed up for the exchange, you can send your Bitcoin straight to the other exchange. Remember, just copy the wallet address where you want your coins to go and paste it into the wallet where you hold the coins. Send, verify with two-factor authentication, and complete any other verification processes. That's it.

The example below shows the Binance Deposit Address you will copy.

Some exchanges often provide a link with a transaction ID. Click the link and you'll see the transaction progress. It might take up to an hour.

That's really about it. Once the transaction is confirmed, your money is on Binance, and you can invest in Ripple, or any other coin you want.

SOME TRICKS ABOUT TRADING BETWEEN ALTCOINS

We don't want to forget these awesome tricks, so we're just going to list them here.

AFTER YOU USE SOME BITCOIN TO INVEST IN AN ALTCOIN

If you don't want to invest all your Bitcoin in Ripple, you can invest it in other coins—or you can move the Bitcoin to an offline wallet, so it's off the exchange and can only be accessed with your private keys (and stored somewhere safe).

TRADING BETWEEN TWO ALT COINS (NOT AS HARD AS YOU MIGHT THINK)

Okay, so now you have Ripple and want to trade it for Electroneum (ETN) or Wax Token (WAX). Can you do that on an exchange like Binance?

Hmm . . . yeah, sort of. You'll have to sell Ripple back to Bitcoin, then buy the new coin with Bitcoin. It's two trades instead of one. Otherwise, it's pretty simple.

TRADING DIRECTLY FROM COIN TO COIN

A more interesting way to trade directly from coin to coin is called Atomic Swaps. It's an evolving area, not quite available to the public yet.

REDUCING YOUR TRADING FEES (USD VS. STABLE COIN)

Of course, you may also want to exchange your Bitcoin back to fiat from time to time. When people first start out, they don't realize that trading Bitcoin back and forth to USD (or other fiat) comes with really high fees—in large part, because fiat currencies are not cryptocurrencies and cannot be directly traded. This means every time you want to sell Bitcoin to buy USD (as an example) you're paying the higher banking fees for making traditional banking transactions.

If you want to reduce your trading fee costs, here's what you do. Instead of trading your Bitcoin for USD, you can trade it to USD stable coins—USD Tether (USDT), for example.

As mentioned earlier, stable coins are cryptocurrency coins backed by fiat currency. Otherwise, they're no different from any other coin you trade on a cryptocurrency exchange. For you, that means the trading fees are a fraction of the price. So, if you're paying 3% in Bitcoin to fiat, you can expect to pay 0.05% to as low as 0.01% for Bitcoin to USD Tether.

As a reminder, the exchange where you bought your Bitcoin may not have the Bitcoin to fiat exchange services available. Many exchanges provide services to buy Bitcoin via wire transfer or credit/debit card, but they may not have a facility to trade back to fiat. When this occurs, you'll need to move your Bitcoin to another exchange that provides these services so you can return back to fiat as required. Again, the fees are higher for doing this, so we recommend doing it only when necessary.

THIS IS THE BIT WHERE WE TALK ABOUT TAXES

Now that you've made some trades, you'll have gains and losses to go with them. That's where the taxman questions come up, every time.

To get you started, when it comes time to file, you can download a complete list of all your transactions from the exchanges where you traded.

After that, it can get complicated and messy. For example, here are a few questions you may be asking yourself when it comes time to report on taxes:

- Do I have to pay taxes on micropayments (like buying a coffee with Bitcoin)?

- If I sell Bitcoin to a stable USD coin, is that treated as a taxable event?

- If I use Bitcoin to buy a coin, then sell the coin back to Bitcoin, is that a taxable event?

- If I make a profit in USD but actually lost Bitcoin in my transaction, is that seen as a gain or loss?

As always, it's best to get some good tax advice and make sure you double-check that advice too. The problem: every country taxes cryptocurrency differently. Not only that, the rules are constantly updating and changing. So as much as we'd love to cover this topic in greater detail and provide you the right information, we want to make sure you get this right and report it the right way. Whatever you do, don't guess and don't try to do it without help.

CHAPTER THIRTEEN

WHAT DOES THE FUTURE HOLD?

I magine a world where companies and governments are more transparent and held to a higher standard. We'd have access to the information that enables us to better decide where to put our money and how to vote. Believe it or not, blockchain technology can help. It's so exciting to think about all the possibilities!

It might not be long before blockchain impacts everything we do. Our homes, cars, cities, governments, and even our own bodies can be improved and made more efficient using blockchain technology. And we're not talking about the distant future with robotics and 3D printing on Mars. There are some immediate and near-term problems that blockchain can help solve.

With that, here's a fascinating look at where we are and where we might go. Who knows? It just might help you identify potential investment opportunities that could have some very positive outcomes in the future.

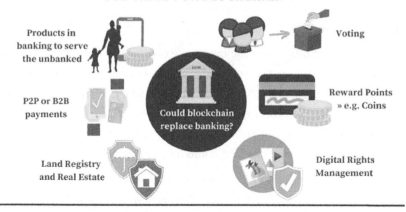

Products in banking to serve the unbanked

Voting

P2P or B2B payments

Reward Points » e.g. Coins

Could blockchain replace banking?

Land Registry and Real Estate

Digital Rights Management

Look at any big tech company, from Facebook to Google, and they all have the same problem—the security of their user's data. Who controls that data, who has access to it, and on what level? Simply being able to control your data with the blockchain gives the power back to you, the user.

We bet you're curious how this will affect other areas of your life, because data privacy is only the beginning!

CARS

Today, when it comes to our cars, we tend to track everything in a hand-written logbook stuffed in the glove compartment—if we keep any record at all (which many of us don't).

But imagine if every car had an onboard computer with its own blockchain that could store data and not be tampered with. If you bought a used car, you would know if that car was in an accident. Nobody could play around with the odometer or the service record. You could more accurately keep track of replacement parts and better understand the history of the car when utilizing the blockchain.

Of course, as with any good advancement in technology, there's often a tradeoff or some unforeseen consequence to consider. Blockchain will be no exception.

In this case, think about the insurance companies getting their hands on your car's data. On the surface, it seems harmless; but what if that data was so precise it kept track of whether you're prone to speeding, reckless driving, or pushing your car too hard? Would your insurance rates go up? As a potential buyer of a used car, data like that can be useful; but in the wrong hands, it could be used against you.

Information can be an incredibly powerful tool, so it all comes down to who has access and how that information is used. Luckily, with blockchain technology, we control our data and determine who can access it. You shouldn't be required to share it in order to gain access to services.

By the way, this isn't even the future of the auto industry we're talking about—it's happening now. This is one aspect where Tesla is ahead of the game. Every Tesla is connected to a network that gathers data based on your driving habits and the car's performance. The cars are continually getting smarter. With all that data, they can make better and more efficient cars. We hope to see more of that kind of positive influence.

SMART HOMES

Right now, we only know what we're being charged when we get a bill at the end of the month—and we have to take the word of the utility companies.

Think of all the things in your home that could be recorded on the blockchain to give you better insight into your costs and usage: gas, electric, water, landlines, mobile phones, and the Internet, just to name a few. Blockchain technology could even take it a step further and predetermine when a repair is needed. For example, it might get to the point where you can track every single electric outlet in your house to spot potential inefficiencies and problems.

How about this? You have a way to purchase replacement parts ahead of time and have them delivered when something needs to be fixed—no more going to the store for light bulbs or having to call a plumber at the last minute.

Everything could be done automatically (with your authorization). That means a personalized blockchain could potentially help you save money and prevent problems before they even occur.

SMARTPHONES AND PERSONAL DEVICES

What about your smartphone and computer—do you really know how they're tracking data usage on any of your devices. Do you know how much data is being used on your phone and why? There's no transparency whatsoever. You don't know what's driving the data transmission back and forth. You only know if you've exceeded a certain number of gigabytes per month, and you have to take the service provider's word for it. Our idle devices are often using data without us even realizing it. Wouldn't it be nice to be more in control of all our data and usage of it? There's no reason you couldn't have that data made available to you openly and transparently.

DIGITAL GAMING

Some games have specific in-game purchases where players can buy and upgrade digital items. Marketplaces and digital exchanges now exist where gamers can trade or sell their digital items with other players both inside and outside of the game. Gamers, in particular, are comfortable with this concept, making blockchain and cryptocurrency-based digital exchange the next logical step for the evolution of gaming.

Since gaming tends to appeal to a more technically savvy crowd, it's the perfect environment for testing out various blockchain services to enhance the gaming and the in-game trading experience.

Imagine using blockchain to enable payments, manage digital assets (collectibles and rare items), trade items, and upgrade items—even track the history of an item or its owners over time. All these features are easily enabled using blockchain technology and cryptocurrency.

In fact, there are already a variety of gaming companies testing out various solutions. Sony is launching a blockchain-based video game on the PlayStation 4; and Epic Games, the studio behind Fortnite, is researching new ways to incorporate blockchain into gaming experiences.

When we say the future of blockchain and gaming is a huge opportunity and will transform the industry, it can't be underestimated.

GOVERNMENT AND POLITICS

When it comes to governments and their typical levels of inefficiency, possibilities abound for how things might change for the better.

For example, the same basic idea for utility bills and monitoring could be applied on a citywide level to root out inefficiencies and equipment failure. It could be expanded to look at traffic patterns, and possibly even interact with the population.

Blockchain could be used to keep our politicians more transparent and accountable. One thing governments are really good at is appropriating large sums of money to different organizations. Whether you agree with those organizations or not is beside the point. With blockchain, there could be an immutable record that informs us exactly where our tax dollars are going.

Just imagine if we were able to democratize and track how our tax dollars are actually being used. We could determine how much money should be spent on certain programs and departments within our community (at a municipal or local level, at least). We wouldn't have to take the government's word for it. We could vote on what we want because blockchain technology could enable us, through consensus, to vote and determine where funds should be allocated, to serve us all better.

With more information comes more transparency and accountability, which could lead to more open debates that eventually bring our communities closer together.

VOTING

We spoke with 2020 presidential candidate Andrew Yang on our show. Being able to vote on the blockchain in national and local elections was a big issue for him. He truly believes blockchain technology can help prevent voter fraud and tampering.

Picture voting the exact same way in every state, local, and national election—no more going to the polls and waiting in line. It would certainly help us avoid issues such as voter suppression, gerrymandering districts, and even issues with hanging chads, as we saw in Florida in a previous election. Honestly, we should be well beyond these kinds of archaic issues by now. We already have the technology to make a move into the digital world that fosters good and positive outcomes for everyone.

Once again, there are safety measures that need to be put in place to give people peace of mind. We don't want people voting multiple times or posing as other people to cast votes. It might require giving everyone an identification number tied to a national database on the blockchain, but we're pretty sure we can achieve these positive outcomes.

RETAIL AND TRACKING THE SUPPLY OF GOODS

In the retail sector, one of the biggest challenges is managing inventory, which starts with suppliers, transportation, and resellers, and ends with the retailers themselves. When it comes to stock and managing returns, the whole process can get very messy. It doesn't have to be this way. Blockchain is perfect for retail and businesses that rely on tracking inventory.

You may be wondering if this already exists. The simple answer is no.

Companies use a lot of complicated technology to do basic integration. Some of the bigger companies have great internal systems. But when it comes to the flow of information between companies, all of whom build their own systems their own way, it's an entirely different problem.

Now that we have blockchain, we could build a more efficient way for companies to share, transact, and track transactions between each other, with full transparency. Remember, when we said this is Internet 3.0? This is our opportunity to use blockchain to create a decentralized way to transact with each other. No need to overcomplicate it.

HEALTH CARE

It's so easy for things to get overlooked and fall through the cracks in many health care systems. Whether looking at the various government-run health care programs around the world, or even the private insurance model in the United States, blockchain technology could be utilized to more accurately keep track of data.

Consolidating your medical records and prescription history to a (private) blockchain ledger could streamline the process and pave the way for a more accurate, transparent, and safer health care system.

Think of wearable devices—instead of big tech companies selling our data to insurance companies, data from our wearables could be controlled by us and, when desired, sent to our doctors and health care professionals.

You could use blockchain technology to monitor your health continually, to root out potential illnesses and diseases before they become a problem.

One day, we might have tiny robotic devices inside our bodies that keep track of our organs and bodily functions—internal wearables as it were. Let's say you have an artificial heart, and it's connected to a blockchain. It could compile data so your doctor or cardiologist could use it to get a clearer picture and determine the best possible care. If doctors could more accurately track your medical care, it would significantly improve their diagnosis and treatment while also better allowing them to detect problems early.

These types of advances could help you live a healthier life while keeping your personal medical information more private. And there are already projects focusing on artificial intelligence and blockchain being used together—something to keep an eye on for future investment.

LOYALTY POINTS

Loyalty programs operate by providing you points in exchange for shopping or using their services; they include airline miles and retail shops, even coffee.

SINGAPORE AIRLINES

Singapore is one of the crypto capitals of the world so it's no surprise Singapore Airlines is getting involved as well. The airline announced they're implementing their loyalty program, KrisFlyer, into a blockchain after a six-month trial. The idea is to provide passengers with a digital wallet that will store their points, or miles, to use for shopping or purchasing tickets. They're basically replacing points with coins, which is an innovative idea.

Can you imagine using a digital wallet to manage your rewards? You could either use a single token to manage all your loyalty programs or have a digital wallet with a variety of tokens accessible on your smartphone, where you store all your coins for each place you collect points. No more keeping track of reward cards. It seems the logical next step, and likely not far from reality.

BANKING THE UNBANKED

Did you know, globally 39% of adults don't have a bank account? In regions such as sub-Saharan Africa, only 34% have a bank account; and in the Middle East, only 14% have a bank account.

It may sound crazy, but it's true.

In many regions in the world, users cannot get bank accounts or verify their identity (the process called KYC or Know Your Customer) because they don't have a birth certificate or any form of national ID. Sometimes the closest bank is too far away to visit. These issues not only prevent people from having banking services, they prevent them from having the ability to purchase land, property, or access basic life or health insurance.

If you're wondering how blockchain could help, consider this: anyone who has a smartphone can download apps, including wallet apps where you can store your coins. Once you have apps, services, and money all in one place, the limitations you have today can be removed.

Just think of the doors that could open up for so many people around the world.

THE FUTURE OF GLOBAL TRADE

Consolidation, simplification, efficiency, and transparency are some of the many ways blockchain and cryptocurrency can help us learn and evolve as a society. Just look at where we came from less than two hundred years ago.

There was a time in the United States (before the Civil War) when there were 8,000 different currencies. Yes, 8,000! There was gold and silver, of course, but since the community at large wasn't communicating with each other, each bank created their own currency. Each state had its own currency, the same with corporations. It wasn't long before inflation took off. Nobody knew if a Sears buck was worth more than a J.P. Morgan buck or a buck from the Commonwealth of Massachusetts (who, by the way, were the first to come up with paper money).

It's interesting that corporations like J.P. Morgan once created their own currency and have now created their own cryptocurrency. It's come full circle. What's even more interesting is how there is a parallel between the evolution of traditional currency and what we now see unfolding for cryptocurrency.

Perhaps no aspect of our world economy could benefit more from that universal currency than global trade.

Granted, there's a common currency every country uses for trade today: the US dollar. But it still creates some limitations between countries. So, imagine if there was a single coin or trading currency that was neutral and not governed by a country.

That doesn't mean we'd have to do away with borders or debts. Economies would still operate the same as they do today. Some countries would be more expensive to live in and visit than others, just like they are today. There would just be more transparency and efficiency.

Take BRICS, for example. BRICS is the acronym for the trade organization involving five emerging economies: Brazil, Russia, India, China, and South Africa. Currently, they trade between each other using US dollars. To do so, they must sell their own currency to buy USD; they use the USD to buy goods from the other country; the other country then sells the USD to buy their own currency. Even though this is very inefficient, they have to do this because their currencies do not have direct trading pairs with each other.

In response, the BRICS nations have been considering a BRICS coin, which would allow them to trade directly with one another, using a common (digital) currency. It would give them unrestrained free trade without any additional currency trading. It would also remove any potential intervention or control of the currency used.

There are so many opportunities to build new products and services, create greater efficiencies, reduce fraud, and give us the control of our money and data in such a way that we have a form of universal financial freedom globally.

CHAPTER FOURTEEN

AN INVITATION FOR YOU (AND GRANDMA)

When we first started with cryptocurrency, we didn't know anything. To be honest, we had our doubts. But the more we learned, the more we recognized the potential. We believe that blockchain technology and Bitcoin will continue to gain more and more mainstream adoption over time.

We wrote this book so you might have a chance to get involved before your grandma does. Hopefully, the world of blockchain and cryptocurrency is no longer quite as mysterious as it once was.

Blockchain and cryptocurrency is no different from any other emerging technology—it's faced with people either quick to dismiss or too intimated to learn something new. Even the Internet, Amazon, and Facebook suffered from misunderstandings that lead to years of naysayers claiming it would go nowhere. Thankfully, there are always people willing to take the time to understand these new technologies and explore all the possibilities. There are always companies wise enough to invest in something new to expand, adopt and grow their businesses. With these realities, it's clear Bitcoin, cryptocurrency, and blockchain aren't going anywhere.

You've seen how a blockchain environment is far more secure, efficient, and accurate than the traditional banking system.

Sure, it still requires a certain level of trust. But that's true even with traditional banking—perhaps even more so, since they can ultimately shut your accounts or lock you out of your funds. With blockchain and cryptocurrency, your funds are always safe and always in your control. Financial transactions no longer need to be constrained by a country's border. Money goes to whatever address you send it and shows up within minutes, anywhere in the world.

You have a solid foundation with which to understand what's really going on.

You'll begin to see "Bitcoin accepted here" posted in shops and on websites as a sign blockchain and cryptocurrency is evolving at an even faster pace than Facebook. When cryptocurrency is mentioned in the news, you'll know the real story. You'll be able to join conversations you might otherwise have just tuned out or avoided altogether. And you'll begin to identify investment opportunities in both traditional businesses and cryptocurrency projects when you see ways in which blockchain can positively impact our daily lives.

Now that you've read the book, you've taken the first step to ensuring you will not be left behind. You'll be able to hold your head up high and show your grandma a thing or two about blockchain, cryptocurrency and Bitcoin, before she beats you to it.

To learn more, check out the additional content on our website, www.beleftbehind.com and subscribe to our podcast/YouTube show, *The Coin Chat.*

THE END

APPENDIX

Steve and Yuri

- **Book Website:** https://www.beleftbehind.com/
- **Email:** Authors@beleftbehind.com
- The Coin Chat
  - **YouTube:** http://bit.ly/BLBYouTube
  - **Spotify:** http://bit.ly/BLBSpotify
  - **iTunes:** http://bit.ly/BLBITunes
  - **Stitcher:** http://bit.ly/BLBStitcher
  - **Amazon Flash Briefing:** http://bit.ly/BLBAmazon

Wir Bank

- https://www.wir.ch/

Bitcoin Whitepaper

- https://bitcoin.org/bitcoin.pdf
- https://bitcoin.org/en/

Calculate Your Bitcoin in USD

- https://99bitcoins.com/satoshi-usd-converter

Companies accepting Bitcoin (and more ways to spend your Bitcoin)

- **Profit Trailer (Automated trading software):** http://bit.ly/BLBPT
- **Moon (Shop with Crypto):** http://bit.ly/BLBShop1
- **Spedn (Spend cryptocurrency with mobile):** http://bit.ly/BLBShop2

- Lolli (Shopping Online): http://bit.ly/BLBShop3

- Expedia (Travel): http://bit.ly/BLBExpedia

- Microsoft Xbox (Gaming): http://bit.ly/BLBXbox

- Overstock (Shopping Online): http://bit.ly/BLBOverstock

- Coffee in Prague (Paralelní Polis Bitcoin Coffee): http://bit.ly/BLBPrague

- All the crypto ATMs and cryptocurrency merchants on a map: http://bit.ly/BLBATM

- Virgin Galactic (Space Travel): http://bit.ly/BLBSpace

- CheapAir (Travel): http://bit.ly/BLBFLY

- Dish (Pay TV with Satellite): http://bit.ly/BLBDISH

Debit/Credit Cards to Spend Bitcoin and other coins

- Wirex: http://bit.ly/BLBWirex

- Change: http://bit.ly/BLBChange

- BitPay: http://bit.ly/BLBBitPay

Social Networking

- Minds.com: http://bit.ly/BLBMinds

- Libra: http://bit.ly/BLBLibra

URLs Purchased by Amazon in 2017 (but may not be working)

- https://amazonbitcoin.com/

- https://amazonetherum.com/

- https://amazoncryptocurrency.com/

- https://amazoncryptocurrencies.com/

Software Wallets

- **Crypto Compare:** https://cryptocompare.com/wallets
- **Blockchain:** https://blockchain.com/
- **Jaxx Liberty:** https://jaxx.io/
- **Exodus:** https://exodus.io/
- **MyEtherwallet (MEW):** https://www.myetherwallet.com/

Hardware Wallets

- **Trezor:** https://trezor.io/
- **KeepKey:** https://shapeshift.io/keepkey/
- **Ballet:** https://www.balletcrypto.com/
- **Cryptosteel:** https://cryptosteel.com/
- **Ledger:** https://ledger.com/

Blockchain Explorers

- **Bitcoin Explorer:** https://www.blockchain.com/
- **Ethereum Explorer:** https://etherscan.io/

VPN Software

- **Orchid:** https://www.orchid.com/
- **Private Internet Access (PIA):** https://www.privateinternetaccess.com/
- **Nord VPN:** https://nordvpn.com/
- **Express VPN:** https://www.expressvpn.com/

Cryptocurrency exchanges

- **Binance:** https://binance.com/

- Binance Jersey (Fiat to Cryptocurrency exchange): https://binance.je/
- Bitmart: https://bitmart.com/
- Bittrex: https://bittrex.com/
- Coinbase (Buy & Sell Cryptocurrency with Fiat): https://coinbase.com/
- Gemini (Buy & Sell Cryptocurrency with Fiat): https://gemini.com/
- ZB.com: https://www.zb.com/
- ZBG: https://www.zbg.com/
- UPbit: https://sg.upbit.com/home
- Exrates: https://exrates.me/
- BCEX: https://www.bcex.ca/
- HitBTC: https://hitbtc.com/

Coin Market Cap Websites

- CoinMarketCap: https://coinmarketcap.com/
- CoinPaprika: https://coinpaprika.com/
- CoinGecko: https://www.coingecko.com/en
- World Coin Index: https://www.worldcoinindex.com/

News Sources

- Yahoo Finance: https://finance.yahoo.com/
- Google Finance: https://finance.google.com/
- Hacker Noon: https://hackernoon.com/
- Medium: https://medium.com/

Note: there are many cryptocurrency and mainstream news sites as well

LIST OF TERMS

Altcoin - Any cryptocurrency coin other than Bitcoin, which was the original cryptocurrency.

Atomic Swaps - To trade directly from coin to coin.

Blockchain - This is a distributed ledger secured using cryptography.

Cold storage - Storing cryptocurrency away from the web in a wallet or another storage mechanism to increase security.

Confirmation - When a transaction has been verified by miners and added to the blockchain.

Consensus - Reached when all network participants approve the validity of the transactions.

Cryptocurrency - This is a type of digital asset used as a medium of exchange in business transactions.

Exchange – A web-service that allows customers to exchange virtual currency into various assets such as fiat to cryptocurrency or cryptocurrency to cryptocurrency.

Fork - This term applies to a blockchain that's split into two separate chains, normally to accommodate new governance rules.

Fiat currency - Any currency that's issued by a government or a central bank.

Hardware Wallet - An actual device that looks like a USB flash drive. It's a type of hardware device with firmware. You plug it into your PC (in the USB port) and it allows you to access your coins offline.

Halvening - Bitcoin has a total supply of 21 million coins that will be slowly released (mined) over time. Approximately every four years, the number of Bitcoin "mined" is reduced, or halved. (The process of mining is what releases the coins into circulation).

Mining - This process uses computer hardware to solve complex mathematical problems and decrypt hashes. Miners are rewarded for their work with cryptocurrency coins.

Mnemonic Phrase (Seed Phrase) - When you start with any software or hardware wallet, it provides you with a backup phrase that's typically 12 (up to 24) random words that you have to string together in order.

Paper Wallet – The term used to describe the backup of your wallet addresses, including the process of documenting your passwords, mnemonic phrases, and private keys, to access those wallets.

Private Keys - All your coins are still on the public ledger, but you access them by using your own private key that is linked to your wallet address.

Public Ledger – A chain of blocks on which transaction details are recorded after suitable authentication and verification by the designated network participants.

Satoshi Nakamoto - The founder and creator of Bitcoin, the most popular cryptocurrency. The smallest amount of Bitcoin (0.00000001) is also named after "him." It's called a Satoshi.

Software Wallet - Software you download onto your PC or smartphone.

Stable Coins - Cryptocurrency coins backed by fiat currency.

Tokenomics - How the coin is being used within the DApp or their product or service.

VPN - Creates an encrypted connection between you and whatever websites or apps you're connecting to.

Wallet Address - Addresses consist of between 26 and 35 characters and represent a unique wallet ID on the blockchain, much like a bank account number.

White Paper – A summary of what a project is doing, why they're doing it, their solution, a technical overview, and a roadmap for the project, along with some legal terms.

CRYPTOCURRENCY ACRONYMS AND INITIALISMS

DApps - Decentralized application. Describing a blockchain-based application that operates entirely in a decentralized way.

ICO - Initial Coin Offering. Popular from 2016 to mid-2018, the first way that cryptocurrency projects raised money through crowdfunding.

IEO - Initial Exchange Offering. Popular starting in late 2018 to early 2019, this is a managed crowdfunding model, like Indiegogo or Kickstarter, where the exchanges provide a service for investors to gain early access to invest in project.

HODL - Hold On for Dear Life or meaning "hold". Cryptocurrency slang for holding onto your coins instead of selling them.

KYC – Know your customer. It's how you prove your identity to a bank or exchange.

STO - Security Token Offering. Started in mid-2018 to create a highly regulated environment for high net worth investors to do early investments.

PROJECTS/COINS REFERENCED IN THE BOOK

Bitcoin (BTC): https://bitcoin.org/en/

AmityCoin (XAM): https://www.getamitycoin.org/

Binance (BNB): https://binance.com/

Bitcoin Cash (BCH): https://bitcoin.com/

Cardano (ADA): https://www.cardano.org/

CryptoKitties: https://cryptokitties.co

Dash (DASH): https://www.dash.org/

Electroneum (ETN): https://electroneum.com/

Enjin (ENJ): https://www.enjin.com/

Ethereum (ETH): https://ethereum.org/

Gemini Dollar (GUSD): https://gemini.com/dollar/

Grin (GRIN): https://www.grin-forum.org/

Holo (HOT): https://holo.host/

Horizen (ZEN): https://www.horizen.global/

Komodo (KMD): https://komodoplatform.com/

Litecoin (LTC): https://litecoin.org/

Monero (XLM): https://www.getmonero.org/

PAX (PAX): https://www.paxos.com/pax/

Ripple (XRP): https://ripple.com/

Thetatoken (THETA/TFUEL): https://www.thetatoken.org/

USD Tether (USDT): https://tether.to/

Wax Token (WAX): https://wax.io/

Zcash (ZCASH): https://z.cash/

Made in the USA
Monee, IL
01 October 2021

79202679R00090